# DISTILLATIONS

# DISTILLATIONS

## THE ARCHITECTURE OF MARGARET McCURRY

ORO

# CONTENTS

# A WORK ETHIC UNDER FIRE

by Stanley Tigerman

IN THE SPIRIT OF FULL DISCLOSURE as her husband and her partner, I note that I do not approach the writing of an introduction to a book on Margaret McCurry's architecture objectively. I undertake this task blissfully because I am the one who most closely observes her way of working, ergo I am the one most likely to understand her means and methods of contending with clients and their individual and collective *Mishegoss*.

Margaret comes from a family of architects of various stripes. Her father was—and her sister, her brother-in-law and her husband are—architects all, each with his or her own ideosyncratic approach to the discipline. To break bread at her family's dining table in Lake Forest was to digress about the architectural issues of the day and to debate the impact that those issues might have had on the communal gathering.

Because Margaret was educated in the liberal arts and sciences both in high school and at Vassar College (albeit with a latter dab of professionalism at Harvard University), she brings a Socratic approach to architectural problem-solving. Margaret never sees architecture solely as a vocational field bereft of the more significant issues of the spirit. Her oft-repeated mantra about the need for quiescence in design resonates not only through the spaces between her words but through the spaces defined by the walls of her buildings.

Margaret would never be so bold as to suggest that her work contends with the spirit, but I have no such compunction. Her insistent use of symmetries, both overarching and intimate, situates her directly within the most sacred traditions of architecture. The quality of Margaret's architecture is coalesced somewhere between Shaker reductivist building and craft and her personal interpretation of Mies van der Rohe's minimalist aesthetic as defined by St. Thomas Aquinas, Mies's spiritual guru.

Margaret is renowned for her tenacity. Once she sinks her incisors into a client's calf, nothing can shake her loose. A good architect is often defined as one who has both a long attention span and a high threshold of pain: Margaret is burdened (but her work benefits) by both.

But it is Margaret's personal ethic on which I wish to focus my attention. Margaret is the most ethically inclined architect that I know. She is repulsed by marketing and couldn't identify branding if it popped up right in front of her as she charged forward to her own destiny with connoisseurship. Unlike professionals who do it for money, Margaret is the consummate amateur, if by that definition the prefix *ama* means doing it for love. Margaret's personal code of ethics exudes love while eschewing avarice. Words beggar my admiration for her ethical behavior.

Ours is a time in which professional ethical conduct has been displaced by untrammeled trafficking in commerce. There seems to be no length to which an architect won't go to corral a commission. Margaret belongs to that rapidly diminishing dinosaur class of architects whose inescapable passing will signal the death knell for a profession that fell only too willingly to its knees before the onslaught of free-based capitalism run amok.

Long may she reign.

Stanley Tigerman
Chicago, Illinois, 2011

# INTRODUCTION

by Robert A.M. Stern

MANY OF TODAY'S ARCHITECTS who specialize in single-family houses adapt rural vernacular in a fairly sentimental way. Not so Margaret McCurry, whose forms are fresh and crisp, with razor-sharp details.

With McCurry's hyper-abstraction comes a certain toy-like quality, deliberately invoked in the House of Five Gables but also present to a greater or lesser degree in all of her work. Her houses almost look like the drawings of childhood. Sometimes that is the case of the work of Stanley Tigerman, her partner in life, with whom she shares an office and occasionally shares a project—but while Tigerman's work is redolent of irony and even sarcasm, as Emmanuel Petit will show in a book soon to be published, McCurry's is not. McCurry's houses, which at first may appear as caricature, are anything but: rendered in humble materials, they convey an extraordinary American authenticity. Inside, her houses reveal a very different aspect: her interiors are straightforward, with a Shaker-like austerity amazingly grafted onto a post-Miesian discipline of gridded symmetries.

McCurry's career trajectory is unusual among contemporary architects and goes a long way to explaining her work. Educated at Vassar College, where she majored in art history, McCurry, the daughter of an architect, did not go on to graduate school as one might have expected, but instead joined the Chicago office of the then-powerhouse firm Skidmore, Owings & Merrill, where she worked in the interiors studio for 11 years before sitting for the qualifying examinations that lead to professional certification. For McCurry, this avenue to architectural practice, now no longer open to would-be architects in most states, had much to offer, enabling her to combine a genuine feeling for traditional form with a mastery of Modernist detailing.

McCurry's willingness to tackle relatively modest commissions—mostly houses that are small by today's standards—and pour her all into them is not to be overlooked. For McCurry, houses are not test sites for bigger things: they are the essence of her practice. But the houses are not all. There are stylish interior fit-outs and, more significantly, designs for furniture and furnishings, imaginative to the point of playful but eminently functional.

Throughout all her work, Margaret McCurry gives form to both local and global environments in subtle and clever ways. Her sensibility is clear and direct. Her designs are strictly disciplined, but that discipline is not their raison d'être; it is but an armature on which to construct strong and individual expressions of place, tradition, and character—which is what her work is really about.

Robert A.M. Stern, practicing architect, teacher, and writer, is Dean of the Yale School of Architecture and founder and senior partner of Robert A.M. Stern Architects in New York. He is a Fellow of the American Institute of Architects, and received the AIA New York Chapter's Medal of Honor in 1984 and the Chapter's President's Award in 2001. Mr. Stern is the 2011 Driehaus Prize laureate and in 2008 received the tenth Vincent Scully Prize from the National Building Museum. In 2007, he received both the Athena Award from the Congress for the New Urbanism and the Board of Directors' Honor from the Institute of Classical Architecture and Classical America. He is the author of several books, including Modern Classicism (London: Thames & Hudson; New York: Rizzoli, 1988), The Philip Johnson Tapes: Interviews by Robert A.M. Stern (Monacelli, 2008); and Architecture on the Edge of Postmodernism: Collected Essays 1964–1988 (Yale University Press, 2009). In 1986 he developed and hosted "Pride of Place: Building the American Dream," an eight-part, eight-hour documentary television series aired on the Public Broadcasting System. Mr. Stern is a graduate of Columbia University (B.A., 1960) and Yale University (M. Architecture, 1965).

# FOREWORD

by Robert Campbell

IT'S HARD TO WRITE ABOUT Margaret McCurry's designs because she performs that task so eloquently herself. In the text that accompanies these houses and furnishings, she imagines one house, for example, talking about itself and saying: "I'm not a slave to historical precedent. I'm just giving it an ironic nod." McCurry, of course, is speaking for herself, not only for her house. Her most remarkable quality is her ability to design places that live squarely in the contemporary world while seeming to have evolved out of the traditional motifs we love and understand from the architecture of the past.

Because they are designed to be inhabited by families, the houses nearly always present themselves as aggregations of independent forms, just as a good contemporary family is a collection of independent members. The family members may love to cluster together, but they value their independence too. McCurry's architecture thrives on finding ways to express this sense of the collective presence of autonomous parts. Some of the houses look like piles of cottages. Others make the point with a pattern of small windows that are the architectural equivalent of faces looking out at the world. Every family member is given energetic expression by the architecture.

McCurry understands that architecture is a language, like English, and if you want people to enjoy your writing, you don't write in Esperanto. Her houses are filled with dormers and gables, with what she calls "widow's walk" porches, with person-sized windows and bilateral axes and other familiar "words and phrases" of traditional architecture. But like a creative writer, she makes them new again.

Take as one example the motif of the axis, which Stanley Tigerman mentions in his introduction. McCurry loves to run a powerful visual axis through a house, an axis that seems to magnetize and organize everything it passes, pulling walls and doors and furniture into symmetrical arrangements on both sides. Traditionally, such an axis in a house might terminate in a powerful work of art, or in a hearth and chimney, or in a window with a view of the landscape. McCurry often reinvigorates the axis by making it terminate in all three elements at once. A fireplace may be surrounded by window glass in such a way that the fireplace is framed and presented as if it were a work of art. You get the hearth, the art and the view all at once. It's a poetic collision, an enrichment of architectural language.

No two of McCurry's houses look alike, yet they all have antecedents in the history of architecture. One may play the game of looking like a barn, another like a cluster of fishing cottages, another (one of my favorites) like a blue and white pennant as seen across water. There's pop art here as well as clean-cut Modernist abstraction. One of the

most remarkable is the house that takes as its source the Low House, one of the icons of American architecture. Four garage doors, of all improbable things, become a powerfully expressive element on McCurry's entry façade. It's a stroke of something like genius. Once again, past and present confront each other.

McCurry's work makes nonsense of the silly battle between "modern" and "traditional" architecture. Her book deserves a wide influence.

*Robert Campbell received a Pulitzer Prize for his writing on architecture for the* Boston Globe. *He is the author of a book,* Cityscapes of Boston: An American City Through Time, *of which the* Chicago Tribune *wrote that it "belongs on the bookshelf of anyone who cares about the fate of the American city."*

*Mr. Campbell has been in private practice as an architect since 1975, as a consultant to cultural institutions and cities. He is a Fellow of the American Institute of Architects and the American Academy of Arts and Sciences, and is a former artist-in-residence at the American Academy in Rome. He received the 2004 Award of Honor of the Boston Society of Architects, "in recognition of outstanding contributions to architecture and to the profession." He has taught architectural design at several universities, most recently as Max Fisher Visiting Professor at Michigan. His poems have appeared in the* Atlantic Monthly *and elsewhere, and he has reviewed books on architecture, urbanism, popular culture, and poetry for the* New York Times.

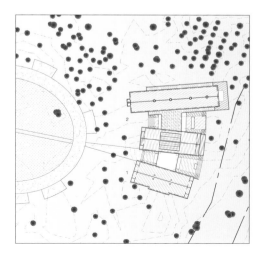

# THE FARMHOUSE

HARBOR COUNTRY, MICHIGAN
1999

**Design Team**
Margaret McCurry, Timothy Green

**Interior Designer**
Margaret McCurry and Owners

**Lighting Design**
Tigerman McCurry Architects

**Landscape Design**
Stan Beikmann, Beikmann Associates

**Landscape Architect**
Maria Smithburg, Artemisia Landscape Design

**General Contractor**
Dunes Development

**Photographers**
Steve Hall, Hedrich Blessing Photographers
Timothy Hursley

**Honors**
Chicago Chapter American Institute of Architects, Distinguished
Building Award, Citation of Merit, 2000

**Publications**
*Architectural Digest*, "Remaining Faithful: A Rural Retreat Stays
True to Its Time and Place," June 2002
*The Farmhouse*, by Jean Rehkamp Larson, Taunton Press, 2004

"Margaret recognized what we wanted, and
we gave her carte blanche. The house works
very well – and it's a fun place to be."
—Client, *Architectural Digest*, June 2002

16

Compelled by sentimentality and the knowledge that the former owners (a farm family) would be retained to work the land, Chicago clients commissioned the architect to convert this 26-acre Michigan farm into an expanded family compound while preserving as much as was practical of the original farm house.

This modest 1½-story structure was crudely constructed. Metal clapboard covered the original simulated brick asphalt shingles, and the 8-foot ceilings on the first floor were oppressive. The land rose at the rear of the house, where assorted outbuildings in varying stages of disrepair peppered the landscape. The most disreputable crowded close to the farmhouse blocking expansion to the rear. After serious soul searching, it was agreed that these crumbling structures would be taken down and the most reusable, which were aligned along an east-west axis, would be saved.

The most reasonable reuse of the low-ceilinged existing farmhouse was as a bedroom wing. The old house was stripped down to its original 2x4 wood frame and new symmetrically disposed window openings were created. Two guest bedrooms with baths were designed to fill the first floor as lofts with accompanying baths for grandchildren and were constructed in the attic. A new master bedroom was hyphened from the main house by a flat-roofed section that gave one loft a deck and access to a playhouse in the bedroom attic. A variance permitted the 4-foot extension of a porch into the front yard engaging the existing gable.

This form set the proportions for the rear addition of a 1½-story great room bridged by a steel walkway to the sixth bedroom tucked above the living room and overlooking the sunroom and screened porch. The original ridge beam was reinforced to support this new cross gable. The choice of modest practical materials such as radiant heated concrete floors and stock stainless-steel kitchen cabinets completes the Midwestern metaphor. Corrugated metal panels clad the complex, and were vertically placed on the new, horizontally on the old. The whole is covered in checkered asphalt shingles carrying on a local tradition of eccentric roofing. Packed into 3,500 square feet, the old/new farm shelters another family while putting food on neighborhood tables.

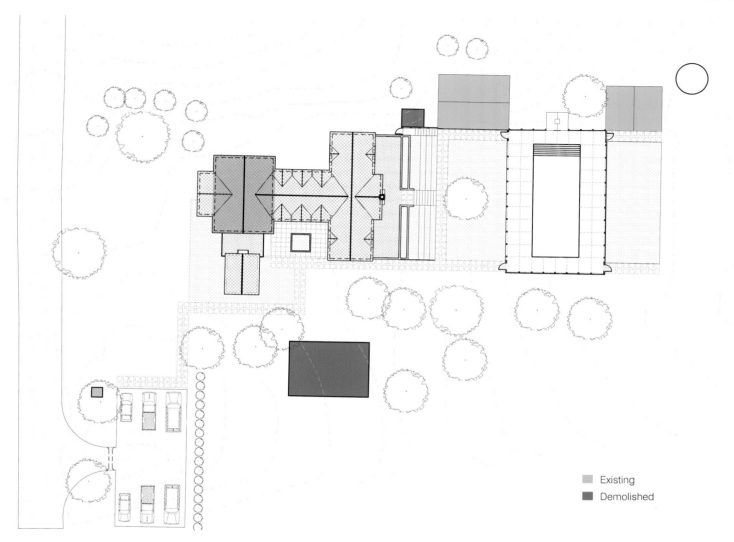

Existing
Demolished

Site Plan

0    10          40
  5      20

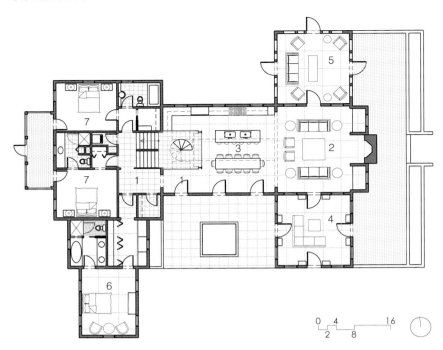

1   Entry
2   Living Room
3   Kitchen & Dining
4   Sunroom
5   Porch
6   Master Suite
7   Guest Bedroom & Bath
8   Bunkroom
9   Bridge
10  Upper Deck
11  Playroom

First-floor plan

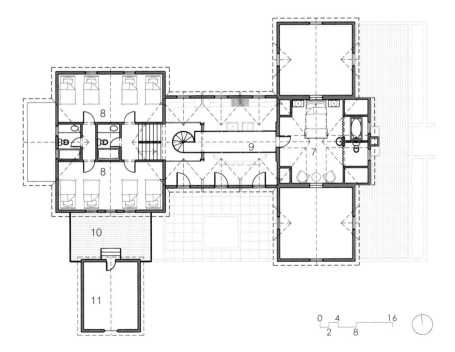

Second-floor plan

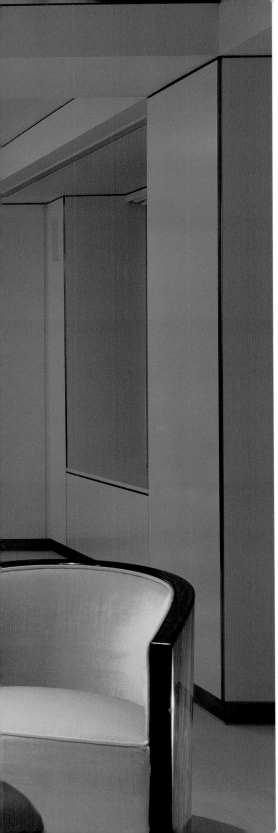

# FOUR SEASONS

CHICAGO, ILLINOIS
1998

**Design Team**
Margaret McCurry, Rocco Castellano

**Interior Designer**
Margaret McCurry, Melany Telleen

**Lighting Design**
Sylvan R. Shemitz, Elliptipar
(formerly Sylvan R. Shemitz Design, Inc.)

**General Contractor**
Tip Top Builders

**Photographers**
Steve Hall, Hedrich Blessing Photographers
Christopher Barrett, Hedrich Blessing Photographers

**Publications**
*Architectural Digest,* "Spatial Relations: Creating a Complete
Environment in a Chicago High-Rise," April 2003

*"Everywhere I look I see something beautiful –
every detail is worked out."*
—Client, *Architectural Digest,* April 2003

Our clients, a couple in their 70s, assembled two adjacent apartments in a multi-use condominium complex designed by the New York firm of Kohn Pederson Fox at the end of the "magnificent mile" in Chicago. Connecting the two two-bedroom units was a challenge, primarily due to the arbitrary disposition of plumbing risers and mechanical systems and a non-modular structural system. For example, to attach the master bath to the master bedroom caused the architect to circumnavigate one of two immovable HVAC/laundry areas, which was accomplished through a series of corridors whose intersections and termini became opportunities for the display of art and antiques.

Programmatically, one of the charges was to design a 3,000-square-foot museum-like modern interior that would blend a collection of old and not so old master drawings, and French Art Deco furniture with new furniture designed in that mode and veneered in macassar ebony. Another was to maximize storage throughout, particularly in the dining room, where a large china collection was to be housed. A third was to prioritize views and maximize ceiling heights – understandable, given an 8'6" slab to slab. This dimension, of course, shrank due to a raised limestone floor elevated to cover pipe bends and to accept the prerequisite acoustical material, and a lowered plaster ceiling concealing conduit, sprinkler runs and miniature can lights.

To counteract the potential oppressiveness of low ceilings in an open plan, we compartmentalized the ceilings, subdividing areas by means of "mechanical" beams in the dining room. These clad "beams" rest on cabinetry "columns", thus solving both visual and storage issues. All details were of diminutive scale and all reductive materials were revealed with a 3/8" stainless-steel angle set into quirk miters at the corners. 3/8" stainless panels case deep doorways and 3" stainless sheeting clads the base. The delicate detailing balances the precise proportioning of the rooms. A classical order prevails, created by localized symmetries, poché passageways and en-suite rooms within a contemporary aesthetic. This partnership produces a counterpoint between present and past, thus enriching sensory experience.

The husband is retired from his profession of banking and finance. The couple travel extensively and collect art and antiques, are affiliated with several museums and are involved in charities associated with AIDS and Alzheimer's disease.

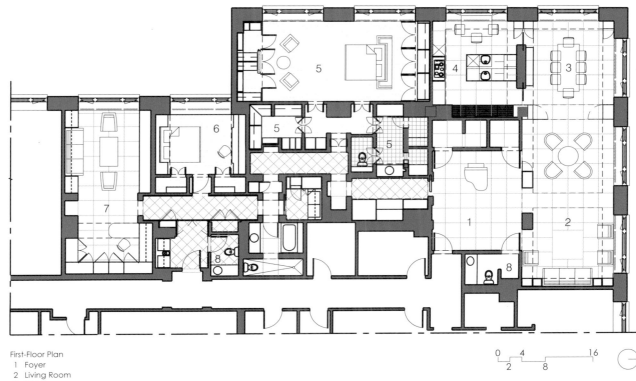

First-Floor Plan
1  Foyer
2  Living Room
3  Dining
4  Kitchen
5  Master Suite
6  Guest Room / Her Office
7  Den / His Office
8  Powder Room

```
0     4        16
  2       8
```

In this foyer powder room, a remote wall-mounted spout sends water through a stainless-steel trough recessed in the glass countertop to spill into the glass bowl, thereby amusing guests and grandchildren alike.

Axial corridors that circumnavigate a utility room to connect the two apartments become focal points for art and antiques at the end of their axes.

Above: Glass shelves display Lalique vases collected in Paris while across the corridor a mirror image frosted glass panel borrows light from the master bath and vice versa.

# HICKORY BUSINESS FURNITURE

HICKORY, NORTH CAROLINA
1998

**Design Team**
Margaret McCurry, Melany Telleen, Dong Huy Kim

**Photographer**
Jim Hedrich, Hedrich Blessing Photographers

**Honors**
IIDA, IFMA NeoCon Gold Award, Furniture System Design for HBF, 1998

**Publications**
*Contract Design*, "A Place of Her Own," September, 1998
*Elle Décor*, "Corporate Makeover: HBF Reinterprets the Office,"
October, 1998

*"The Charette Collection provides a graceful way to embrace, contain and conceal technology, while the Cache Collection of seating reveals the Designer's reverence for tradition and a refined sense of what is functional and modern."*
—Client, 1998

The Charrette & Cache Collections are McCurry's response to HBF's commission to create a private executive office collection that transitions between the past and the present with an eye towards the future. HBF believed the furniture line should personalize the work space in contradistinction to the trend towards hi-tech mobile environments that are efficient but not always friendly as they forswear linkages with historical precedents.

The name of the Charrette collection is derived from the French word for cart, which at the École des Beaux-Artes in Paris was the vehicle that, when wheeled past drafting boards at the architecture school, signaled "times up" for students who were then required to place their finished projects on the cart for review by the professor. Today, architectural practices all use the term "on Charrette" as a metaphor for being on a deadline, and so the Charrette Collection naturally refers to its architect creator.

Inspiration for the desk and credenza assembly came from two classic archetypes. A tiny 18th-century French desk spotted at an antique show became the demi-lune drop-leaf "desk with cartonnier." The curved miniature cabinet with pencil drawers and tambour door sits at the end of the racetrack top and rotates to face inward or outward as the occasion arises. Its counterpart, the credenza or traditional secretaire, is a modern interpretation of the roll-top desk. Its camel-back shape flares upward to create a central niche for the ubiquitous computer. The two curved side doors, when open, reveal spaces for additional technological equipment while their back sides become pin-up surfaces.

The seating ensemble designated as the Cache Collection is a distillation of furniture designed during the European Art Deco movement of the early 20th century. The gently flared back and arms, at once crisp and softly sculpted, are a hallmark of that elegant era. The fully upholstered lounge chair or bergère, with short tapered legs, is available both as a complement to the sofa or settee and in a lighter upholstered version set on a taller wood frame. Yet another variation, the side chair or fauteuil, with its tailored open frame, can be used either in a corporate office situation or as a residential dining chair as the architect in her interior design for the Double Low House. A trio of fabric lines in the French fashion named Carte Blanche, Tête-à-Tête and San Soucis accompany the Cache Collection. All are woven of worsted wool in subtle patterns with unique color combinations that reflect McCurry's favorite palette rather than current coloring trends.

The intention of the entire collection was to refashion historical forms into a transitional grouping that while solving contemporary workplace issues would convey a sense of permanence and civility in the office environment.

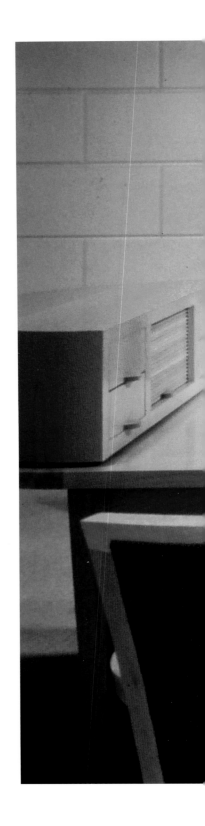

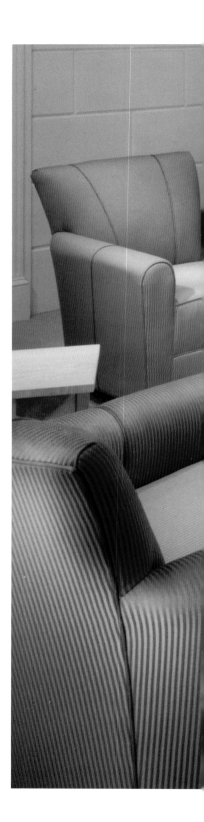

# PENTHOUSE

CHICAGO, ILLINOIS
2000

**Design Team**
Margaret McCurry, Melany Telleen, Lisa Kulisek

**Interior Design**
Margaret McCurry, Melany Telleen

**Lighting Design**
Tigerman McCurry Architects

**Landscape Design**
Doug Hoerr, Hoerr Schaudt Landscape Architects

**General Contractor**
Blackmore Construction

**Photographer**
Steve Hall, Hedrich Blessing Photographers

The architect was engaged to renovate and update this penthouse residence in one of the stately old brick and limestone buildings overlooking Chicago's Lincoln Park. The residence, which encompasses the entire sixth and seventh floors, includes extensive terraces at both front and rear of the living space. At the east, opening out on the park, the façade steps back behind an existing limestone balustrade flanked by two pergolas, creating a private aerie. At the rear, a newly planted terrace extends back 40 feet over the existing fifth-floor living space. Walkways and trellis structures, as well as plantings selected for year-round interest provide a rare urban backyard. A smaller paved terrace at the seventh floor is located over the unit's' kitchen and dining spaces, and incorporates the building's elevator penthouse, as well as a view down onto the sixth-floor garden.

Work on the 5,000-square-foot residence involved opening up, via two pairs of new French doors, views and access onto the new west terrace, a relocation and expansion of the kitchen, and a redefinition of the series of public spaces making up this floor. The entry sequence was revised to create a private foyer exterior to the residence – at this foyer, a bench is provided for visitors to remove their shoes prior to entering. In the living room, an existing masonry wall section was removed and replaced with a pier that was in turn encased in a wood surround. This restructured column aligns with a new row of faux columns beyond designed to separate the living room from circulation space, thereby allowing the living room and the adjacent sitting room to read as distinct spaces.

Fixtures and finishes throughout both floors were redone – existing flooring was replaced by maple planks, and maple veneer was used to clad columns and the curving walls of the newly reconfigured stair connecting the sixth and seventh floors. The stair, with an inset handrail, is intended to read as a solid wood insert into the white interior. Custom radiator covers were fabricated to integrate the existing heating system into the architecture. Though the original configuration of rooms remained after the renovation, head heights at doors throughout were raised to align with existing window heads, and particularly on the upper level, openings into rooms were modified by infilling existing and providing new relocated openings to provide a more cohesive layout to the rooms and the connecting spaces. The master bath was completely reworked, and in contrast to the maple used in the remainder of the spaces, water-resistant mahogany was used for the wood vanity and tub surround. The mahogany is repeated in the cable-hung bed designed for the space.

The architect was initially retained for this work by a young married couple in 1998, and has continued to this day to revise and refine the residence – the addition of three children has had its effect on the program and furnishings, though the spaces remain essentially unchanged.

First-Floor Plan
1   Foyer
2   Living Room
3   Den
4   Study
5   Dining Room
6   Kitchen
7   Outdoor Terrace

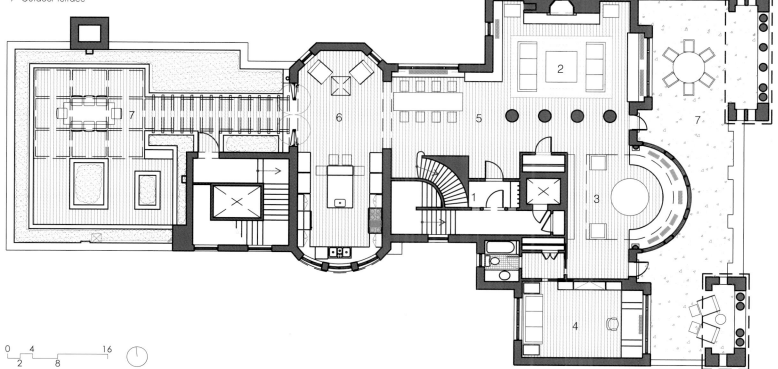

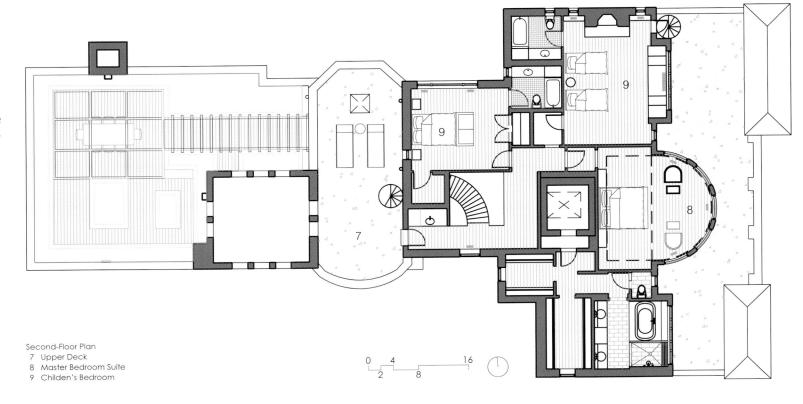

Second-Floor Plan
 7  Upper Deck
 8  Master Bedroom Suite
 9  Childen's Bedroom

# DOUBLE LOW HOUSE

THE NORTH SHORE, ILLINOIS
2001

**Design Team**
Margaret McCurry, Jeffery Phelps, Lisa Kulisek

**Interior Design**
Margaret McCurry, Lisa Kulisek, Lauren Coburn

**Lighting Design**
Tigerman McCurry Architects

**Contractor**
Eiseland Builders

**Photographers**
Steve Hall, Hedrich Blessing Photographers
Christopher Barrett, Hedrich Blessing Photographers

On a half-acre corner lot with the restrictive floor area ratio (FAR) and zoning setbacks typical of Chicago's suburban North Shore, our clients requested a residence that primarily revolved around family relationships. It was to comfortably coexist in a community of "historic" structures both old and new while creating its own, uniquely informal persona. The appearance of four garage doors on the front façade speaks to the traditional carriage house forecourt while the two-story foyer and axial fireplace reinforce the grand country house format. The site's rear yard shares a remarkable vista across three neighboring yards and was the exposure to which all rooms aspired. And so, on the first floor, rooms march enfilade from the master suite through his study with its golf ball display, the family room with his piano and on through her kitchen culminating in her private study. This plan promotes family interaction with him, a busy corporate executive, yet also provides a private retreat for her, a community-active housewife.

In the spirit of congeniality, the children are provided with an upstairs common room as well as a below-stairs media center and exercise facility including his driving range. Her separate garage serves as a discrete drop-off for groceries and unruly puppies whose fenced dog run abuts the mud and flower facility. Tile floors on the first level add a practical element while the Aga stove in the kitchen, like its Swedish counterpart, exudes warmth throughout the day and night, eschewing the need for extra fossil fuel consumption.

Dubbed the double "Low" house in reference to the iconic McKim, Mead and White single reverse gable house built for the Low family of Bristol, Rhode Island, (since demolished), the two reverse gables shelter a plethora of rooms with the perception, especially frontally, of only a few. The FAR for such a structure dictated that second-floor areas over 7 feet in height be less than 50% of the size of the first floor, thereby necessitating some artful roof pitching. Covering over 7,000 square feet on three floors, the house settles gracefully and quietly into this small suburban lot, granting all family members spaces in which to assemble as well as disassemble.

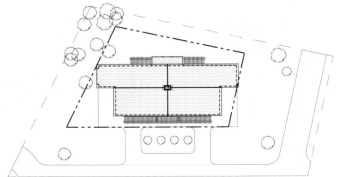

First-Floor Plan
1  Foyer
2  Living Room
3  Dining Room
4  Kitchen
5  Her Office
6  Mudroom
7  His Office
8  Her Dressing Room
9  Master Bedroom
10  Master Bath
11  His Dressing Room

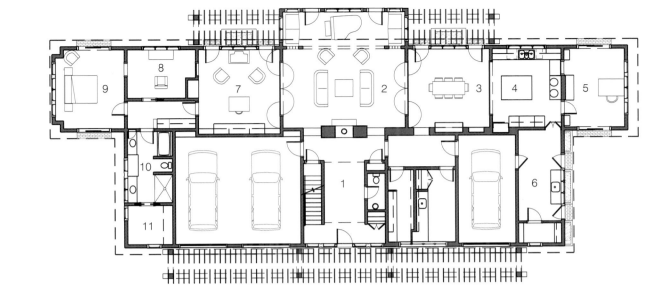

Second-Floor Plan
12 Second-Floor Foyer
13 Common Room
14 Guest Bedrooms

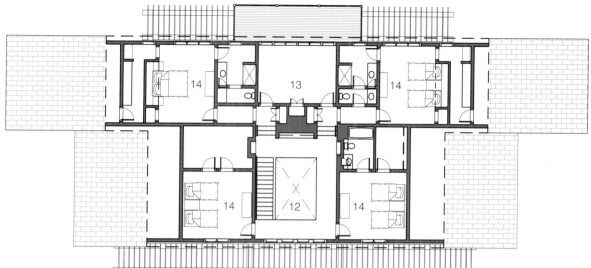

# WATER TOWER CONDOMINUM

CHICAGO, ILLINOIS
2001

**Design Team**
Margaret McCurry, Stanley Tigerman, Lisa Kulisek

**Interior Design**
Margaret McCurry, Stanley Tigerman, Lisa Kulisek, Lauren Coburn

**Lighting Design**
Sylan R. Shemitz, Elliptipar
(formerly Sylvan R. Shemitz Design, Inc.)

**General Contractor**
Tip Top Builders

**Photographer2**
Jon Miller, Hedrich Blessing Photographers
Christopher Barrett, Hedrich Blessing Photographers

**Publications**
*Architectural Digest,* "A Dual Endeavor in Chicago: Life and Art
Deftly converge at Water Tower Place," March 2004

66

The clients, a mature, well-traveled couple relocating to Chicago's Water Tower Place from a family home in Des Moines, commissioned the architects to design a museum setting for their diverse collection of old masters, antiquities and modern crafts. Two separate apartments totaling 5,800 square feet, were to be combined and gutted. The program called for: a suite of rooms for themselves and a separate guest suite adaptable for future live-in help; and spaces for extended family functions as well as extensive entertaining, to include many auxiliary places such as a pantry, wine cellar, dark room and study.

The architects chose to create a plan not unlike that of a traditional museum with axial progressions of rooms arranged enfilade to extend spatial perceptions. The building, the first of Chicago's retail/ hotel/ residential complexes presented a series of design challenges. The association no longer permits any relocation of electrical, plumbing or mechanical chases or risers. At the 70th floor there is considerable building movement and deflection in the floor slabs. The 8'8" ceilings are radiantly heated, thus precluding any penetrations, and the windows terminate at the ceiling plane, causing air distribution systems to be pulled back from them to avoid obscuring views.

The design strategy was to establish a secondary datum line at 7'8" to allow space for mechanical, fireproofing and sound systems, as well as conduit and low voltage transformers, and to distribute conditioned air, sprinkler heads, and speakers through a continuous aluminum grille, which also acts as a reveal to absorb movement. To gain a perception of greater height, especially necessary in larger rooms, the bronze anodized aluminum window bays are extended vertically by cladding the sills and surrounds as well as the wall below in the same material. Hope's bronze doors with translucent glass- divided lights slide from pockets or swing from bronze hinges, reiterating that material palette while providing the effect of shoji screens requested by the clients, who admire traditional Japanese architecture and desired the same sense of serenity.

Display systems were reinvented for different collections. Of the two bronze silk-paneled walls in the living room that oppose each window bay and echo their coloration, one is further subdivided into squares studded with bronze plugs that permit expansion of the African mask collection. New furnishings that the partners designed, such as metal or glass lounge kitchen or dining tables, needed to join the previously established eccentric craft tradition and to be completely unique in concept.

For example, Tigerman's square glass living room display table is cleaved by an arc that echoes the curved light track above and the terrazzo floor divider below, which in turn is "traced" through the carpet by a dark line that divides two textures. The lounge seating is composed of modern classics selected for their strong simple shapes that act as foils for the complex craft, as do the neutral fabrics and hand-woven carpets. All new pieces were carefully chosen to relate to the old and to contribute to a harmonious relationship between art and architecture.

Floor Plan
1　Foyer
2　Living Room
3　Library
4　Video Room
5　Master Suite
6　Dining Room
7　Pantry
9　Kitchen
9　Family Room / Office
10　Guest Bedroom Suite
11　Photo Studio
12　Photo Gallery

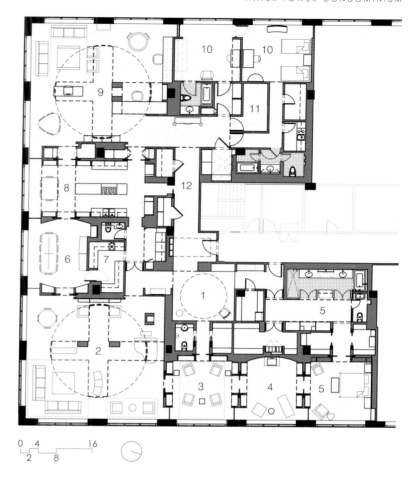

0　4　　　16
　2　　8

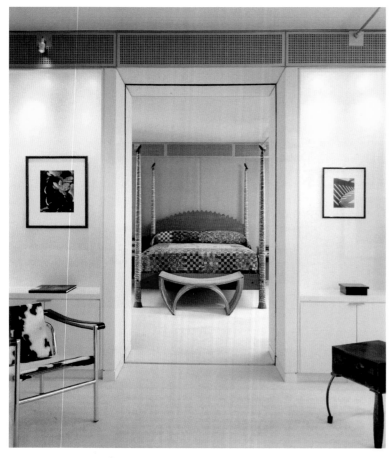

# THE HOUSE OF FIVE GABLES

SOUTHWESTERN MICHIGAN
2001

**Design Team**
Margaret McCurry, Kimberly Carroll, Kevin Stephenson

**Interior Design**
Margaret McCurry with Owner

**Lighting Design**
Tigerman McCurry Architects

**General Contractor**
Norman Graham

**Photographers**
Steve Hall, Hedrich Blessing Photographers
Timothy Hursley

**Awards**
ALA Design Awards, Silver Medal, 2003

**Publications**
*Architectural Digest,* "Midwestern Abstraction: Distilling the
   Essence of the Barn on Lake Michigan," May 2005
*Architectural Digest,* "AD 100: Margaret McCurry," January
   2007
*Dream Homes Chicago,* pgs. 237-238, Panache Partners, 2007
*Lakeside Living: Waterfront Houses, Cottages, and Cabins of
   the Great Lakes,* by Linda Leigh Paul, Universe Publishing, pgs.
   35-39, 2007

Perched atop a sandy knoll and surrounded by the forested dunes that define Lake Michigan's Eastern Shore, this 3,100-square-foot country home for Chicagoans is a modern reinterpretation of the farm structures that populate this rural region of Michigan. Like a "push-me, pull-me" toy, two identical "barn"/blocks slide symmetrically, forward bracketing the middle block that slides backward, thus permitting maximum exterior exposures. Three gables form the roof of each block while two more matching gables terminate the cross axes. The axial plan creates vistas from inside to out and vice versa. The focal point of three primary axes is a fireplace – the hearth, symbolic of home, while the verso view is into the hinterland.

Sited amid five deeply wooded acres, the home's fenestration patterns have an important function in lightening the interior. The same windows that are combined in transparent grids on the ground floor act as single monitors on the upper level to capture the sunny days that are less frequent here in the lee of the Great Lake. Inside the spare luminous spaces. lusty natural materials (local riverbed stones and hickory wood floors) create a warm counterpoint to the abstraction of cool dematerialized white walls. Minimalist furnishings contribute to feelings of serenity and essentiality.

Practical industrial materials reinforce the Midwestern rural aesthetic. Clad in vertical tongue and groove cedar siding, the "barns" are painted in not the typical "barn red," but, a bright pure red that simply says, "I'm not a slave to historical precedent. I'm just giving it an ironic nod." Standing seam galvanized steel roofs shed melting snow safely held by snow guards. Aluminum-clad windows and woven wire stair rails and deck enclosures add to the maintenance-free industrial format. These taut compilations of archetypal "barns" become the culmination of a city dweller's dream – a tranquil forest retreat far from the maddening crowd.

*"It is not often that a new style appears in American domestic architecture, but architect Margaret McCurry recently made it happen... this lakeside house combines vernacular references with McCurry's consistent Miesian classicism in plan."*
—Mildred F. Schmertz, Architectural Digest, May 2005

*"... [The house] has personality! The house is so clean, crisp and captivating. It charms me and embraces me at the same time. It seems to rise up from the earth with such strength – and I personally feel a sense of renewal with each visit."*
—Client, a letter to the architect, August 2000

0 10 40
5 20

Site Plan

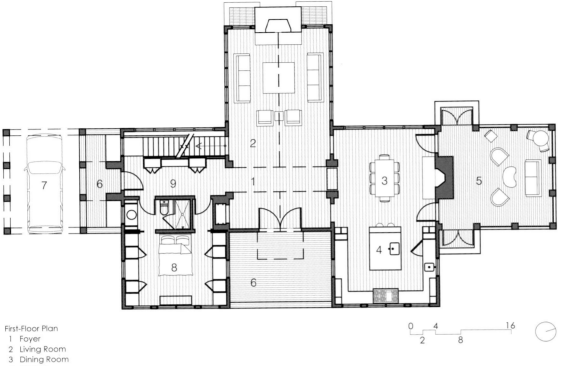

First-Floor Plan
1  Foyer
2  Living Room
3  Dining Room
4  Kitchen
5  Screened Porch
6  Deck
7  Carport
8  Guest Bedroom Suite
9  Mudroom

0   4        16
  2      8

Second-Floor Plan
10 Stair
11 Guest Bedroom Suite
12 Bridge
13 Master Bedroom
14 Upper Deck

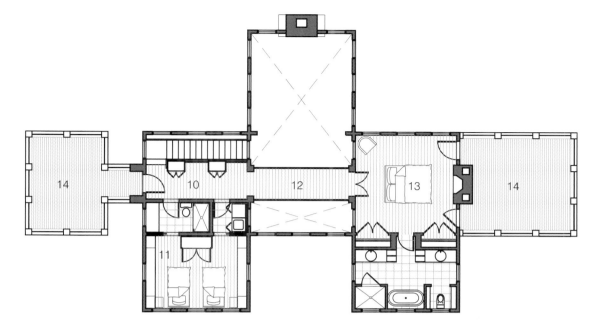

0   4      16
  2    8

# THE BLUE HOUSE

HARBOR COUNTRY, MICHIGAN
2003

**Design Team**
Margaret McCurry, Sidsel Just, Jeremy Hinton

**Interior Design**
Margaret McCurry and Owner

**Lighting Design**
Tigerman McCurry Architects

**General Contractor**
Burlingame Builders

**Photographers**
Steve Hall, Hedrich Blessing Photographers
Craig Dugan, Hedrich Blessing Photographers

**Publications**
*Architectural Digest,* "Out of the Blue: On the Eastern Shore of
   Lake Michigan, a Home is Memorably Shaped by Color and
   Geometry," June, 2007
*Architectural Digest Private Views: Inside the World's Greatest
   Homes,* published by Harry N. Abrams, Inc., pp. 174-179, 2007

Inserted into the back of the high sand dunes that define Lake Michigan's southeastern shore, this 5,000-square-foot country home for a Chicago family rises 3-½ stories on the street façade to satisfy a program that specified on a 60-foot-wide lot a five bedroom house with all rooms lake-facing. The Michigan Department of Natural Resources' DNR dictated rear yard setbacks from the face of the primary dune and 5-foot side yard setbacks from the county set the perimeters.

By burying slightly over 50% of the lowest level, the architect was able to fulfill the zoning requirements for a 2-½ story structure, which is its configuration on the lake façade. The cross-gabled stair tower that forms the center of the tripartite front façade is offset half a story from the body of the house to mitigate the steep grade change. Flanking the tower two single-car garages are separated and set back to minimalize their street presence while maximizing a central green sward.

This is a modern reiteration of the Midwestern rural vernacular. Sears Roebuck pattern book cottages originated in communities such as this one that stretches along the lakeshore while their counterpart farmsteads filled inland acreage. All were built of native wood. Some expressed their idiosyncrasies, as does this version. Like a barn, this gabled structure is clad in vertical tongue-and-groove cedar siding. Unlike its antecedents, it is painted marine blue, an ironic nod to its lake front setting and a break with precedent. The white standing-seam metal roof, clad windows and steel railings, while practical materials for the site, also reinforce its Navy-esque persona. The small upper-story windows create a wavelike pattern as they flow across the façade. The house sports a continuous white-railed window's walk across its second story. The bedroom doors open onto the balcony, offering access to the "ship's rail." Square awning windows used in gridded combinations or separately enliven the facades and fast-forward the house into the 21st century.

*"This is a house that encourages – one might even say insists upon – engagement with its environment...."*

*"McCurry...knows how to achieve dramatic effects by framing her spaces, forcing the eye to take in various elements one at a time rather than all at once."*

*"McCurry takes great pride in providing what she calls 'little encounters, little surprises' and here they abound."*
—Jeff Turentine, *Architectural Digest,* June 2007

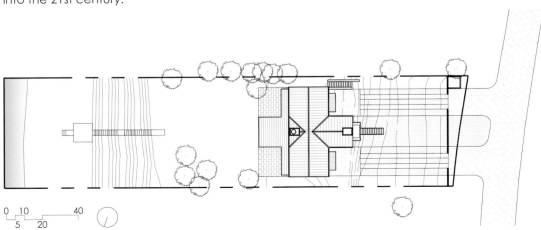

0  10      40
  5    20

Basement-Floor Plan
1  Garage
2  Mudroom & Laundry

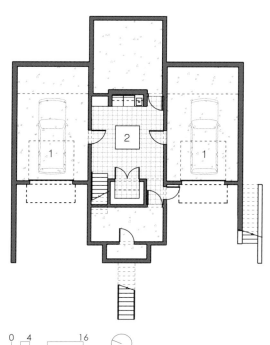

0   4        16
  2     8

First-Floor Plan
3  Upper Deck
4  Master Bedroom Suite
5  Children's Bedroom
6  Shared Bath
7  Stair Tower
8  Sunroom
9  Patio
10  Balcony

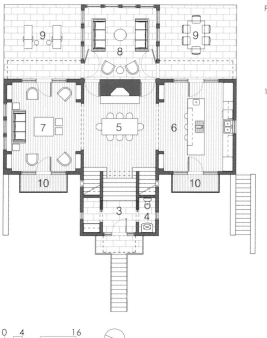

0   4        16
  2     8

96

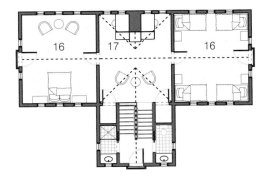

Second-Floor Plan
11 Upper Deck
12 Master Bedroom Suite
13 Children's Bedroom
14 Shared Bath
15 Stair Tower

Third-Floor Plan
16 Guest Bedrooms
17 Family Room

# LAKESIDE COLLECTION

LANDSCAPE FORMS
2004

**Design Team**
Margaret McCurry, Melany Telleen, Joseph Buehler

**Photographer**
Jim Powell, Jim Powell Photography

**Honors**
Interior Design Magazine, Best of Year Award Merit Winner:
Landscape Forms, Lakeside Benches, 2006

**Publications**
*The Boston Globe*, Style Section, "Sitting Pretty," August 3, 2006
*Architect*, "Products," October 2007

The architect was commissioned to create designs for outdoor furnishing that would be not only durable and comfortable but also affordable so that the products would appeal to cost-conscious small and medium-size towns, campuses and public parks across America.

To the casual observer, a bench seems like a pretty simple design proposition. It is, after all, just a flat place on which to sit, sometimes with a back and armrests. The universal folded-steel frame, which recalls the platform swing of another time, is simple, sturdy and economical to fabricate, having a minimum of exposed welds and utilizing stock steel sheets and ¼" bar stock straps. The addition of the decorative embellishments is pure whimsy.

The first of two bench styles has planks of Jarrah wood, a FSC-certified product or Polysite, a synthetic material used in the design of decks, staggered along the back so as to mimic the classic picket fence, a traditional American icon. The second style is a reference to nature itself, with a perforated metal pattern of shoots of grass that grow from tufts on the seat to fronds up the back or a picturesque scattering of gingko leaves blown by the wind. These decorative patterns are incised into steel sheets using state-of-the-art plasma-cutting technology. Backless benches repeat the patterns on their seats. Both designs straddle the line between minimalism and ornamentation, convention and novelty – a delicate balance that is anything but simple; and since they are made entirely of steel, they are totally recyclable – perish the thought!

A complimentary litter receptacle is designed as a trim cylinder with a recessed base available in leaves and grasses patterns.

*"Lakeside is contemporary in form and materials, traditional and pastoral in motifs."*
—Landscape Forms, 2004

# THE CRAYOLA HOUSE

OOSTBURG, WISCONSIN
2005

**Design Team**
Margaret McCurry, Christopher Fein, Jeremy Hinton

**Interior Design**
Margaret McCurry and Owner

**Lighting Design**
Tigerman McCurry Architects

**General Contractor**
Dean Mullikin, Mullikin Construction

**Photographer**
Steve Hall, Hedrich Blessing Photographers

**Publications**
*Architectural Digest,* "A Lakeside Story: Nautical Themes Add
  Whimsy to an Airy House on the Shore," *October 2007*
*Milwaukee Journal Sentinel,* Section N, "Cheerful From the
  Start", October 28, 2007

With its prow pointed towards the waves and clad in sand-proof corrugated steel, this compact 5,500-square-foot waterfront residence for an adman-cum-sea captain and his professorial mate is beached on the western shore of Lake Michigan. It is designed to project a playful, contemporary image constructed with a traditional kit of parts. From the glass block front entry that forms a "hinge" which frames an axial view of the water, to the two cross-axial wings that establish double exposures of both "surf and turf," the house is meant to provide cheerfully practical accommodations for a family of six. This program is reflected in the colored concrete floors that encase radiant tubing for a healthful heating system.

The couple's four sons inhabit four dormered bedrooms tucked under the eaves, while the parents occupy the "bridge," with his and her "widow's walk" balconies shading the lower rooms. The "his and her" theme is furthered by the two separate family rooms below – his with TV for noisy viewing, hers with fireplace for quiet reading. This pair of rooms flank the kitchen, "the prow," which combined with informal dining, was designed to encourage maximum participation in food preparation. The exterior color palette was also a family affair – personally chosen and applied by the captain. The galvanized steel house with its multicolored window frames has become a beacon for fisher folk in their motor boats, often rendezvousing with friends x miles off the Crayola House.

*"I've always loved Margaret's work because it's modern, but not extreme. It's like sculpture you can live in."*
—Client, Architectural Digest, October 2007

*"...Her work is imaginative, sharp and like any exceptional work of art, intriguing. I look at it again and again, yet it always surprises."*
—Harold Levy, a letter to the Editor, Architectural Digest, January 2008

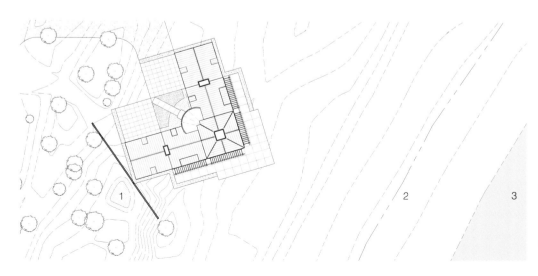

Site Plan
1  Wetland
2  High Water Line
3  Lake Michigan

0  10      40
   5   20

First-Floor Plan
1  Foyer
2  Kitchen & Dining
3  Living Room
4  Screened Porch
5  Den
6  Powder Room
7  Garage

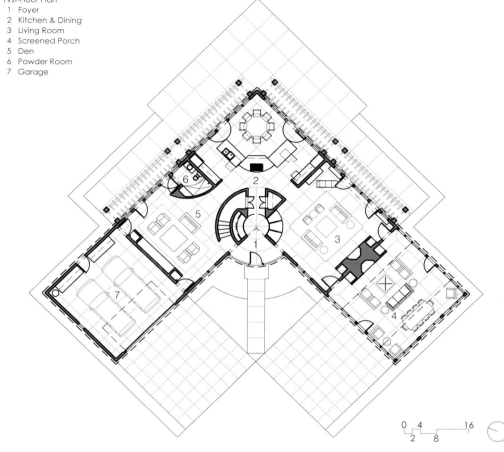

Second-Floor Plan
  8  Stair Hall
  9  Master Bedroom
 10  Master Bath
 11  Guest Bedroom
 12  Balcony

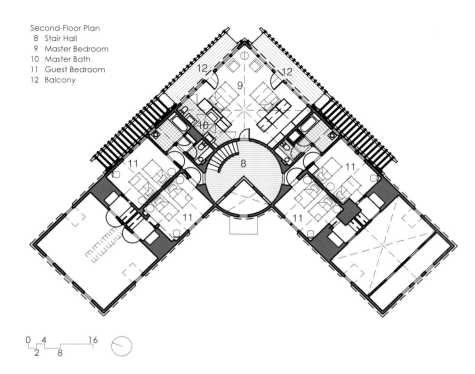

# MID-CENTURY REMODELING

GLENVIEW, ILLINOIS
2007

**Design Team**
Margaret McCurry, Melany Telleen, Phillip Lantz

**Interior Design**
Margaret McCurry, Melany Telleen, Phillip Lantz

**Lighting Design**
Ben White, White Light Designs

**Landscape Architect**
Maria Smithburg, Artemisia Landscape Design

**General Contractor**
Eiesland Builders

**Photographer**
Steve Hall, Hedrich Blessing Photographers

**Honors**
Illinois Chapter ASID, Design Excellence Awards,
   Best in Show, 2008
Illinois Chapter ASID, Design Excellence Awards,
   1st Place, Residential (over 3,000 s.f.), 2008
Dream Home Awards, Best Whole House Remodel
   (over 4,000 s.f.), Silver Award, 2009
Association of Licensed Architects, Merit Award, 2009

**Publications**
*Architectural Digest*, "A Legacy Preserved: Extending the
Life of a Classic Mid-Century Modern for the Generations,"
February 2009

This project consisted of the renovation and updating of a "modern" stone and glass residence in the Chicago suburbs, built in 1953 by Richard Barancik of Barancik, Conte & Associates for the original owners, who wished to remain in the home. The goal was to adapt the home to suit the lifestyles of today, while providing a seamless insertion which would utilize the language of rough stone, expanses of glass, and elegant wood paneling of the original. Increasing the energy efficiency of the original was achieved by reworking the mechanical systems, as well as extending the original radiant floor heating system, providing better R- values and using insulated glazing. A necessary re-roofing allowed for a complete reconfiguration of and addition to the lighting, by a lighting design consultant, which significantly brightened and enriched the interior.

The existing residence, including minor additions done in the late 50s and early 60s, covered approximately 5,000 square feet on a gracious lot of over an acre with a tennis court and swimming pool. Zoning limited allowable impermeable increases to the footprint, but it was deemed essential to keep the house on one level for its elderly owners. The end result was an addition in two parts totaling slightly over 1,000 square feet. Part I consisted of an enlarged and more open kitchen, which included a new opening onto the rear pool terrace, and an expanded breakfast room (projection at west). Part II was the addition of a new sky-lit master bath (far south extension), which included reconfiguring the bedroom corridor to create an axial window and redesigning the bookcases and converting the existing master bath into a closet. Furnishings throughout were also revisited and retuned and art work was relocated.

Tennessee Crab Orchard Limestone was obtained from the original quarry, and craftsmen duplicated the original layout. By reusing the original limestone flooring over an expanded radiant heating system, the green footprint of the residence was increased. The original Paldao wood paneling, a rainforest inhabitant, was supplemented with a sustainable wood, Ovangkol, carefully milled and stained to match the existing. New wood windows were fabricated to stylistically match the original, as was the accompanying bronze hardware. The kitchen floor was redone in terrazzo (a more practical material), custom-blended to complement the limestone flooring. Kitchen, service bar and laundry cabinets are new. All parts of the home were updated with new finishes including carpeting, cork flooring and ceramic tile.

The landscape was redesigned by a landscape architect, including new configurations of plant material. The asphalt drive was removed and the original rose-colored pea gravel reinstituted, which permitted a more environmentally suitable drainage system, as well as a more aesthetically pleasing aspect.

*"I think what Margaret did is seamless. When we walk people through, we have to tell them where the old stops and the new begins. It's much brighter and lighter, and it flows better. It's really the same house, but more beautiful than it ever was."*
—Client, *Architectural Digest,* February 2009

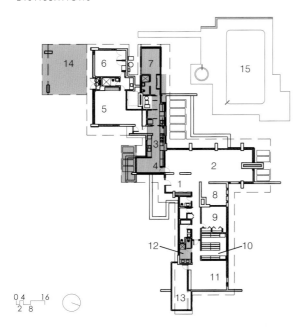

Existing Floor Plan
*Color indicates areas
to be remodeled*

1  Foyer
2  Living & Dining
3  Kitchen
4  Breakfast Room
5  Media Room
6  Guest Bedroom
7  Maid's Room
8  Den
9  Office
10  Dressing Room
11  Master Bedroom
12  Master Bath
13  Deck
14  Carport
15  Pool

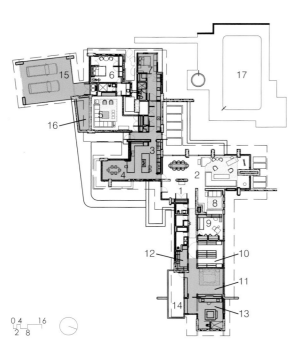

Remodeled Floor Plan
*Color indicates areas remodeled*

1  Foyer
2  Living & Dining
3  Kitchen
4  Breakfast Room
5  Media Room
6  Guest Bedroom
7  Maid's Room
8  Den
9  Office
10  Her Dressing Room
11  Master Bedroom
12  His Dressing Room
13  Master Bath
14  Deck
15  Carport
16  Planter
17  Pool

# THE HOUSE OF A DOZEN DORMERS PLUS ONE

HARBOR COUNTRY, MICHIGAN
2008

**Design Team**
Margaret McCurry, Jeremy Hinton

**Interior Design**
Margaret McCurry, Jeremy Hinton and Owner

**Lighting Design**
Darrell Hawthorne, Architecture & Light

**Landscape Design**
Scott Byron & Company

**General Contractor**
Great Lakes Builders, Inc.

**Photographers**
Steve Hall, Hedrich Blessing Photographers
David Seide, Defined Space

*"...You handled every detail so beautifully and we knew that you would and did create a home that we love and have enjoyed sharing with friends and family."*
—Client, Letter to the architect, Fall 2010

Nestled in a Midwestern forest in Harbor County, Michigan, this shingled country home was designed to accommodate an extended family in a casual setting that would encourage family interaction. The property includes a tennis court with pool house located on axis with the main house, which one approaches by driving through an allée formed by paired garages into a stone forecourt bracketed by walled gardens.

Charged with designing a home that would figuratively embrace visitors approaching the front door, it seemed natural to extend two wings forward to bracket the entrance in just such a welcoming gesture. Crossing the threshold, one immediately looks down the long axis to the warmth of a crackling fire in the great room, which draws one's steps through a gallery past symmetrically paired doorways. The opening on the left leads into the cozy library, which sports its own fireplace while its opposite opens into the stair hall.

Tucking the couple's two children upstairs under the eaves and adding a play room-cum-bunk room for cousins and friends zoned the house such that adult sleeping quarters could occupy each downstairs wing. The southern one allocated for the parents includes a sauna and joint office while the other houses guests. With all the upper story functions located in the midsection of the house, the great room and sun room to the rear enjoy staggered double-height spaces. Following the wood ceiling spline that directs one towards these dramatically proportioned rooms, one passes through the gallery and first encounters the coffered ceiling media center on the left. A French door accesses the terrace while across the way the center's counterpart contains the family kitchen. There can never be too many cooks in this centrally located kitchen. The island doubles as a breakfast bar, kibitzing zone and servery. With the cooktop and range centered on the large three bay windows, stirring the pot is a visual as well as a sensory experience. All appliances are practically clad in stainless steel, which in concert with the greige limestone floors and countertops, becomes a foil for the dark, richly stained white oak that is the primary interior finish.

Positioned above these spaces, the bunk room windows overlook the great room, affording children amusing communication links with family below. Warmed by the radiantly heated stone floors, family and friends dine while looking out into the woods or back towards the Count Rumford fireplace with its sliding screen that runs on rails up the stone façade. French doors flow directly out onto the stone terrace, edged by a White Birch grove. Cocktail hour often transforms the sun room from a quiet, light-filled retreat surrounded by nature during the day to an active gathering spot in the evening. The tall dormered room is lit by a roaring birch fire and an origami fixture, named *Free as a Bird*, designed by the London artist, Eva Menz.

From front to rear, all rooms are aligned on an orderly axis or cross axis that, while directing one's steps, also directs one's eyes through symmetrically disposed doorways into enfilade rooms with axial views into the forest.

Site Plan
1 Main House
2 Garage
3 Pool
4 Pool House
5 Tennis Court
6 Pool Equipment

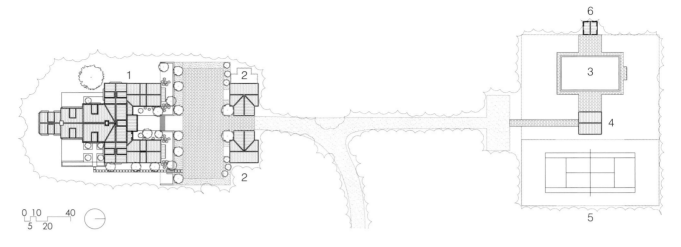

0 10 40
5 20

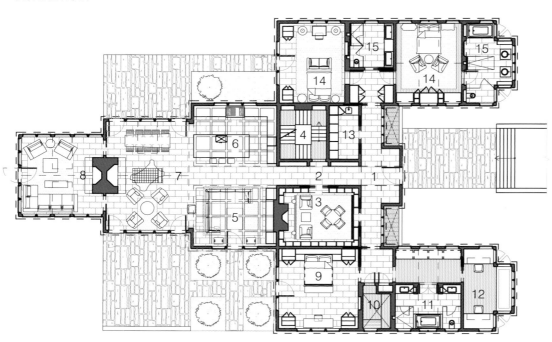

First-Floor Plan
1  Foyer
2  Gallery
3  Library
4  Stair Hall
5  Media Center
6  Kitchen
7  Great Room
8  Sunroom
9  Master Bedroom
10  Sauna
11  Master Bath
12  Office
13  Mudroom
14  Guest Bedroom
15  Guest Bath

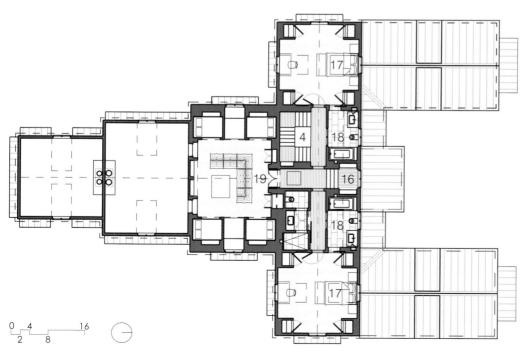

Second-Floor Plan
16 Overlook Niche
17 Child's Bedroom
18 Child's Bathroom
19 Bunk Room

0 4 16
2 8

The glowing windows of the second floor bunkroom seen at left overlook the great room below.

# THE ORCHARDS

HARBOR COUNTRY, MICHIGAN
2008

**Design Team**
Margaret McCurry, Phillip Lantz, Joseph Buehler

**Interior Design**
Margaret McCurry, Catherine Noble

**Lighting Design**
Ben White, White Light Designs

**Landscape Architect**
Maria Smithburg, Artemisia Landscape Design

**General Contractor**
Dunes Development

**Photographer**
Steve Hall, Hedrich Blessing Photographers

**Honors**
Illinois Chapter ASID Design Excellence Award,
   Best of Show, 2010
Illinois Chapter ASID Design Excellence Award,
   First Place, Residential (over 3,000 sf), 2010

**Publications**
*Architectural Digest,* "Theory of Relativity: Soaring
Volumes in the Country Allow a Family to Reach Out
and Connect," June 2009

*"...The house seems to know just who it is, and it claims the land with assurance, taking gentle possession of the surrounding fields."*
—Joseph Giovannini, *Architectural Digest,* June 2009

This is the third project for a Chicago family of five that the architect has completed in the last 12 years. The first the remodeling of a historic duplex penthouse apartment shown earlier was finished in time to welcome their first child. Subsequently, seven years ago she further reconfigured an old clapboard farmhouse ca. 1928 on 30 acres in rural southwestern Michigan that some years before she had remodeled for another Chicago couple. After several years of weekends spent in the old homestead and with the birth of their third child, the couple commissioned her to design and furnish a new house in a former cornfield on the property.

Clad in white corrugated metal with raincoat yellow low e-glass windows, this 7,800-square-foot country home is sited on that 30-acre former truck farm. It takes its architectural inspiration from the white-washed Midwestern vernacular of the region – gable-roofed barns, conical silos and slatted corn cribs. It responds to environmental concerns by using a geothermal field and ground water to heat and cool the house and sun screens to shade the interior. The white metal panels reflect heat during the hot Midwestern summers and brighten the grey winter landscape.

The land as configured by the landscape architect has been replanted with indigenous fruit orchards and a vegetable patch. A pear tree alleé contains a garden parti of native grasses and perennials with a Bertoia sculpture on axis that connects the new house with the remodeled farmhouse, which now serves as guest quarters. A pool complex also designed by the architect to relate to the original homestead now links the two residences. Nature trails encircle the site, which includes a glacially scoured ravine and seasonal wetlands. The children pick wild strawberries in the spring, harvest edible greens in summer and pick from 10 indigenous apple trees in the fall as they learn environmental stewardship.

In response to the family's desire for a warm, practical and interactive interior that is ecologically responsible, all first-floor rooms are interconnected and are clad in quartered American white oak. Limestone floors repel dirt while conducting radiant heat. The master bath shower platform is certified sustainable Ipe. Above the two-story cross-axial atrium, a skylight floods the dining table below with soft diffused light. Second-story bedrooms carpeted in natural sea grass all spill out onto the balcony that shares this light as it surrounds the family eating space below. The staircase rising from this central gathering space is bracketed by a home office and laundry on the second level and borrows light from those rooms. This is a house designed as a serene retreat for its adults as well as a treat for its young children, whose bedrooms each sport lofts for playmates while overlooking the two-story great room, whose fireplaces are Fond du Lac limestone from neighboring Wisconsin. An endless pool provides winter entertainment and exercise while the staircase also leads down to a family play room below. This is a homestead that its family will never outgrow. The young couple plans to retire here in their own nature conservancy and welcome grandchildren some day.

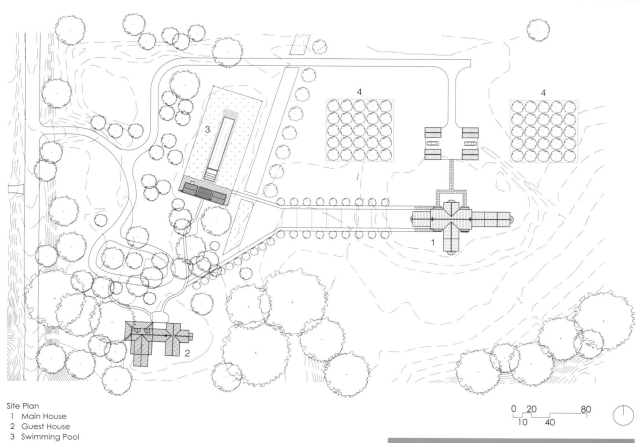

Site Plan
1 Main House
2 Guest House
3 Swimming Pool
4 Orchard

Left: Bracketed by Bradford pear trees, a bronze Bertoia sculpture anchors the flower beds that march along the double allée which connects the pool and guest quarters to the main house.

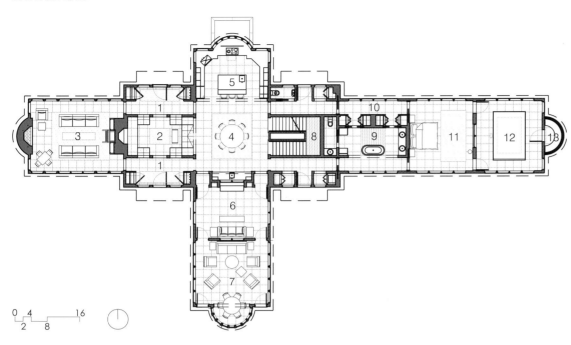

First-Floor Plan
1  Foyer
2  Inglenook
3  Great Room
4  Dining Room
5  Kitchen
6  Family Room
7  Screened Porch
8  Stair Hall
9  Master Bath
10  Master Dressing
11  Master Bedroom
12  Pool Room
13  Steam Room

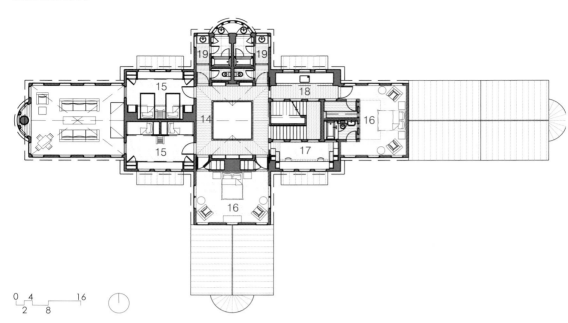

Second-Floor Plan
14  Balcony
15  Child's Bedroom
16  Guest Bedroom
17  Office
18  Laundry
19  Bathrooms

0  4     16
  2   8

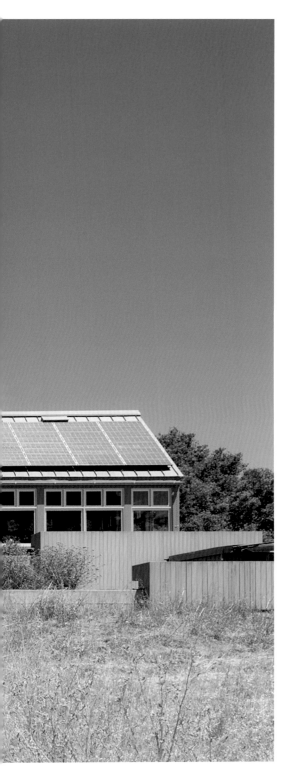

# THE RANCH

SONOMA COUNTY, CALIFORNIA
2010

**Design Team**
Margaret McCurry, Jeremy Hinton

**Associate Architect**
Heidi Richardson, Richardson Architects

**Interior Design**
Margaret McCurry, Heidi Richardson, Jeremy Hinton

**Lighting Design**
Darrell Hawthorne, Architecture & Light

**Landscape Design**
DJ Johns, Zone 17 Landscape Architecture

**Photographer**
Erhard Pfeiffer, Erhard Pfeiffer Photography

**Honors**
ALA, Professional Design Excellence Award of Merit, 2010

Nestled among a redwood ring and the live oak clusters that crown a hill on this 400-acre former cattle ranch in the Sonoma Valley, this 6,000-square-foot house is designed for a family of four. As mandated by the county, the house is carefully sited on its hillside so as to be invisible from across the valley. Environmental concerns as well as county regulations informed the material selection of zinc cladding. Its low toxicity, matte finish and impressive longevity, as well as its ability to heal itself, makes it a major plus for the environment. Solar panels concealed below the hillside heat the domestic hot water, which is sourced from an underground natural spring. Aligned along the south-facing roof, photovoltaic cells are so highly functional that the owners are able to return or sell power back to the grid. All of these sustainable elements make this home completely self-sufficient on its remote hilltop.

The interior cladding from the radiant flooring to the wall and ceiling paneling is farmed birch. The great room was designed for family interactions both within the space and without on the adjacent blue stone terrace that sports a hot tub. The plan also provides for his and her private offices and a sky-lit painting studio for the wife, an accomplished artist. Other amenities include an "endless" swimming pool and sauna geared specifically to a family member with health issues. For this reason also, all rooms on the ground floor are accessible. A steel bridge spanning the great room leads to an overlook where on a clear day, the San Francisco Bay shimmers in the distance, and at night the lights of Santa Rosa twinkle across the valley below.

The landscaping was a concerted effort by the architects and a local landscaper. It complies with local fire codes and uses all native plant material such that the house will settle seamlessly into the land as per the owners' desire to be good stewards of their quintessential Northern California landscape.

*"…I wanted to live inside a sculpture. Margaret,*
*your house is indeed a beautiful piece of art.*
*The house is so strong…I kind of prefer just*
*the house itself… I was realizing that I really*
*prefer to look at all the details inside the*
*house, and to just let my eyes move around,*
*uninterrupted. Your house is enough art for me."*
—Client, Letter to the architect, June 21, 2010

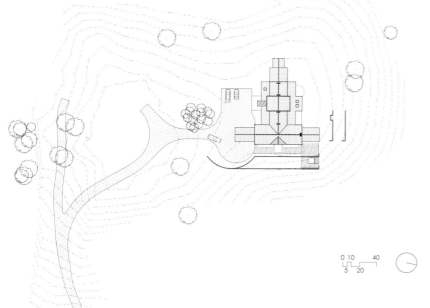

First-Floor Plan
1  Foyer
2  Sauna
3  Powder Room
4  Exercise Room
5  Endless Pool
6  Study
7  Great Room
8  Sunroom
9  Laundry
10  Office
11  Studio
12  Master Dressing Area
13  Master Bath
14  Master Bedroom
15  Sleeping Alcove

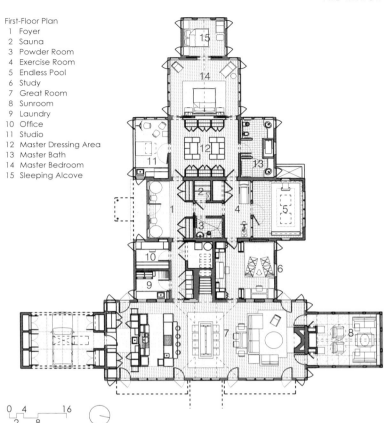

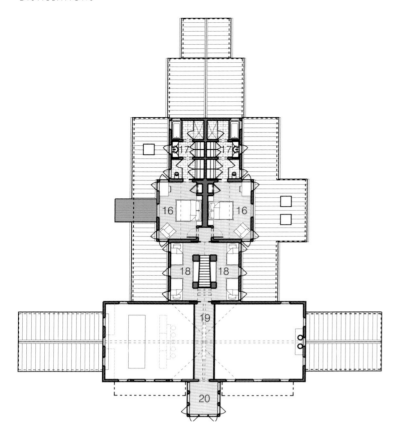

Second-Floor Plan
16 Children's Bedrooms
17 Children's Bath & Dressing Room
18 Guest Bunkroom
19 Bridge
20 Overlook

0  4    16
  2   8

LANDSCAPE FORMS
2011

**Design Team**
Margaret McCurry, John Hooper, Erik Martin

**Photographer**
Jim Powell, Jim Powell Photography

*Windmark seems at once familiar and entirely new. It brings ideas from the past into the present… [The collection] mixes materials and revels in them, combining and juxtaposing them in fresh ways. Precise in form, it has humor and warmth. Highly sophisticated, it is also welcoming.*
—*Landscape Forms: Windmark Collection Catalog*

Following the successful launch of the Lakeside Collection, Landscape Forms asked the architect to expand the outdoor collection to include dining tables and chairs that would appeal to resorts and clubs as well as residences.

A natural evolution of the line was to incorporate scaled-down folded steel strapping for the chair and table frames. The grass and ginko patterns were reconfigured into perforated metal seat and back pans and a third pattern from nature – raindrops was added.

Whereas the benches were deliberately heavy so as to not be removable from their designated sites, the chairs needed to be more manageable – at once heavy enough to not blow away yet light enough to be liftable. This condition dictated that the frame become an aluminum casting but the seat and back remain steel so as to permit the incising of patterns. Bolting the seat and back panels to the frame with stainless-steel hardware permits either to be specified in differing or similar powder-coated colors.

A variety of FSC (Forest Stewardship Council) certified woods were added to the new chair line and would also be available as tabletop planking for the rectangular strap table, whose uniquely configured frame was inspired by an old 19th-century French folding farm table owned by the architect. Round and square versions of the strap frame are available with tops of frosted glass or steel. All tops taper in on their outer edges to effect a lightness and delicacy of detail.

When the architect initially submitted several different chair and table base configurations, a design composed of angled steel sheets welded into either a cruciform-shaped frame or an elongated frame composed of two angles at either end separated by a central spine seemed like another unique design that could be incorporated into the expanded collection. The grass, leaf and rain patterns transferred readily onto these new base configurations. With their folded paper-like forms, it seemed appropriate to call them the Origami Group.

Of sturdy composition on the one hand but of dignified countenance on the other, the artful "Windmark Collection" joins a long line of specialized furnishings designed to grace the landscape.

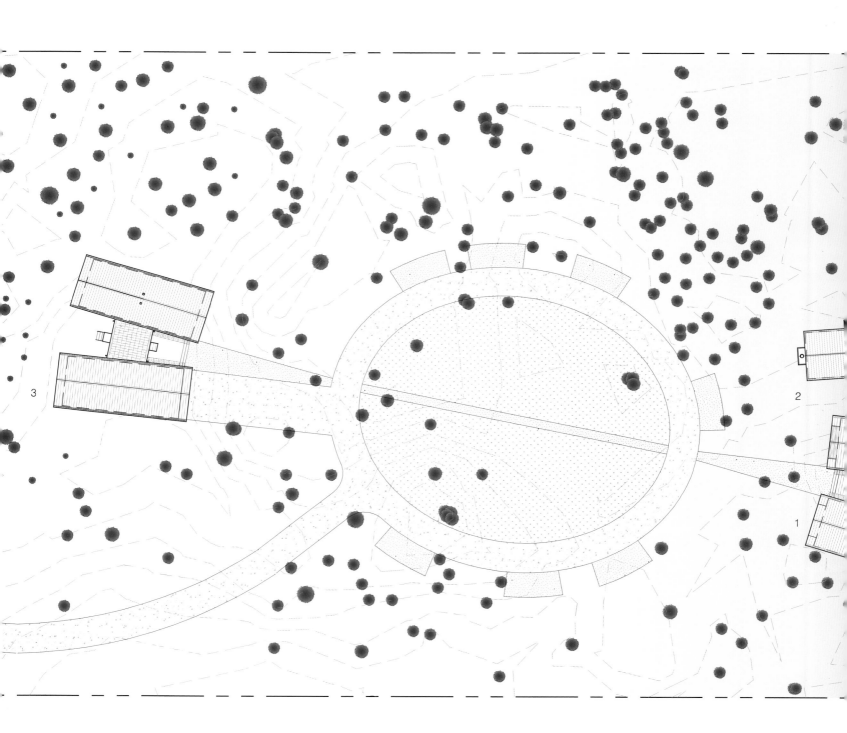

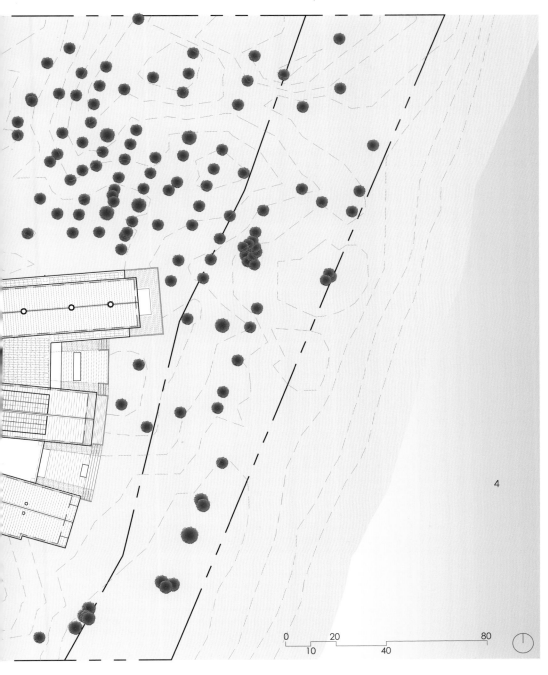

OOSTBURG, WISCONSIN
2011

**Design Team**
Margaret McCurry, Jeremy Hinton, Erik Martin

**Interior Design**
Margaret McCurry and Owner

**Lighting Design**
Darrell Hawthorne, Architecture & Light and Owner

**General Contractor**
Mullikin Construction

4

Site Plan
1  Main House
2  Poolhouse
3  Guest House
4  Lake Michigan

0     20          80
  10        40

Located in a pine and birch forest on the western shore of Lake Michigan, this 8,700-square-foot family compound provides a multifaceted country retreat for a young couple from a Chicago suburb, and their extended families. The clients desired a comfortable yet sophisticated environment to enjoy their summer break and holidays with their five children, family and friends. They contacted McCurry after seeing the Crayola House just a few miles down the beach from their property.

This new Wisconsin retreat has provided an interesting spatial and organizational challenge given the clients' varied program, which includes many guest rooms, bunkrooms, an indoor pool and a separate guest house/garage, as well as both indoor and outdoor gathering spaces. McCurry sited the elements of the house and guest house to create a "pinwheel" off of an open clearing in the forest whereby the program spaces became the "spokes" of the wheel connected by an interior "rim" of circulation, which also provides entry points into the house and axial views towards the lake. This scale-reducing scheme also provides distance between the guest rooms, bunk rooms and the master suite so that privacy is maintained. The house was so placed behind the high water mark that a minimum of the natural vegetation on the site was disturbed as the high water table also dictated a shallow crawl space.

The clients have a great interest in sustainable practices and worked with McCurry to develop strategies to reduce the project's environmental footprint. As a result, the complex incorporates a variety of sustainable features. The homes feature low-VOC foam insulation used in conjunction with cellulose with a high recycled content to achieve a high R-value. A geothermal heating and cooling system, which uses ground water as a heat source, also provides domestic hot water and feeds the radiant floors. In addition, the house uses an area of green roof plantings to capture and control rainwater and to cool that portion of the roof. The house incorporates sunshades that also act as entry canopies, while the low-e windows provide for ample day lighting in much of the house. Most dramatically, a 120-foot-tall tower will support a 10kW wind turbine operating above tree level, which will provide electricity to run the home.

The materials that also play an important role in the design in terms of both comfort and sustainability. A white roof membrane is used on the low slopes to reflect the sun's heat while zinc, an environmentally friendly material occurring naturally and refined sustainably is used as siding and roofing. The cement panels on the foundation and the end walls use a significant amount of recycled material. The interior uses locally quarried Fond du Lac limestone on the fireplaces, and locally harvested northern white pine is used throughout the home on floors and walls with the exception of the pool house, which uses Australian cypress, a moisture-repellent wood. All combine to create a supportive and sustainable environment for the family.

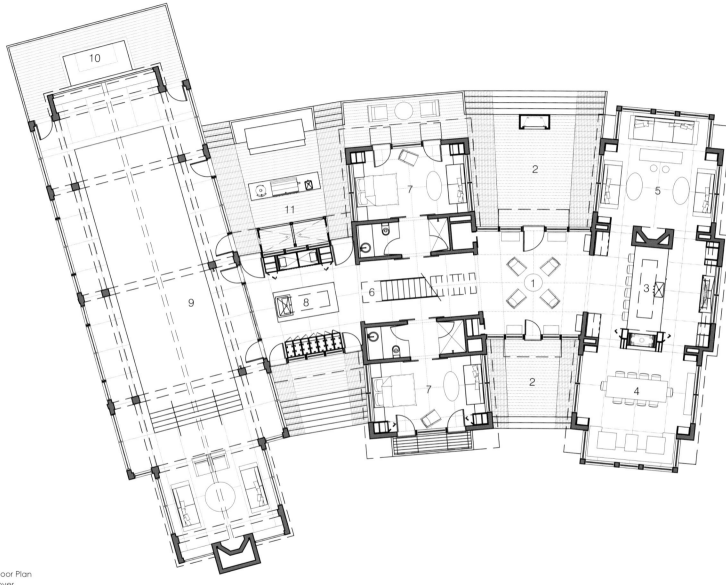

First-Floor Plan
1  Foyer
2  Deck
3  Kitchen
4  Dining Room
5  Living Room
6  Stair Hall
7  Guest Bedroom & Bath
8  Mudroom
9  Poolhouse
10 Hot Tub
11 Cooktop and Picnic Deck

East Elevations

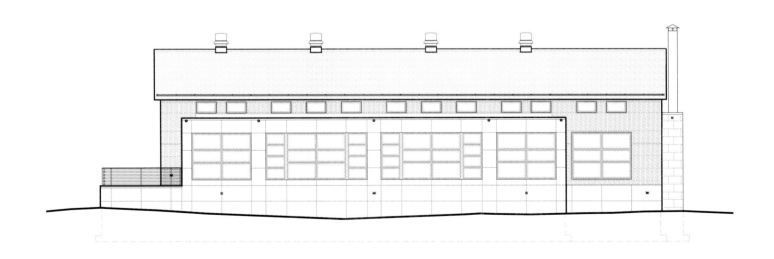

Poolhouse - North Elevation

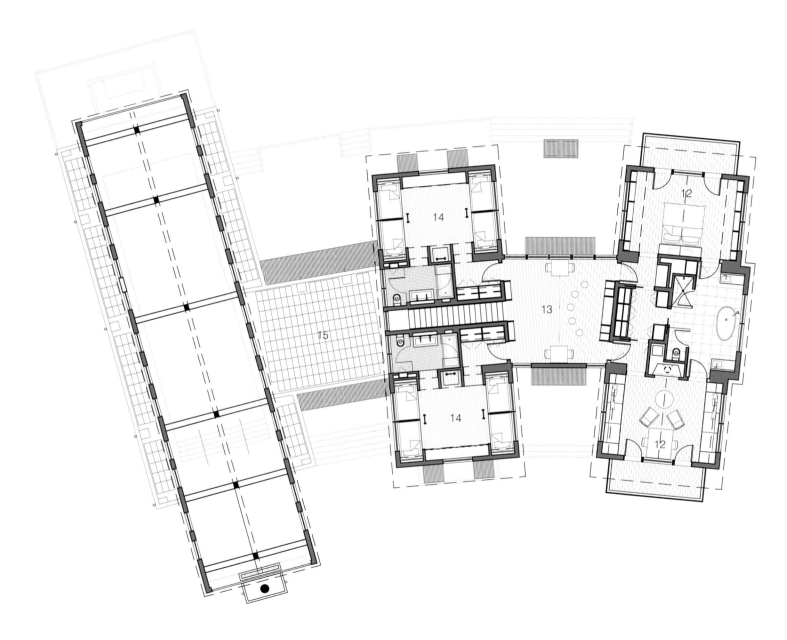

Second-Floor Plan
12  Master Suite
13  Family Room
14  Bunkroom
15  Green Roof

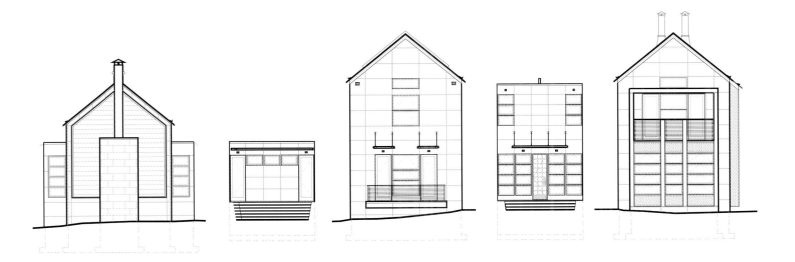

West Elevations

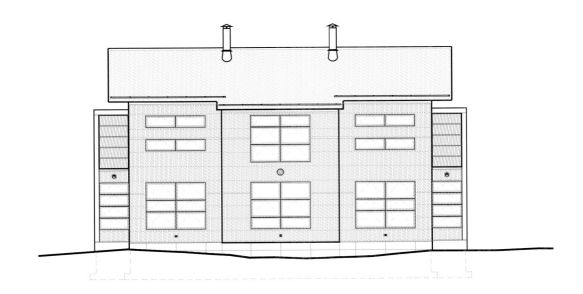

South Wing - South Elevation

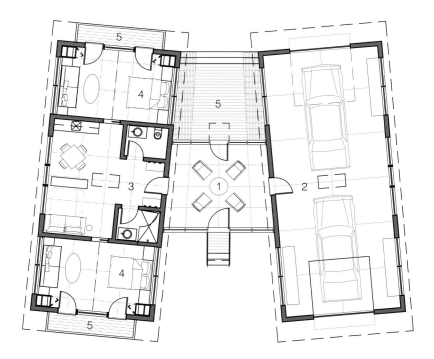

Guest House Floor Plan
1   Screened Porch
2   Garage
3   Living and Dinind
4   Guest Bedroom
5   Deck

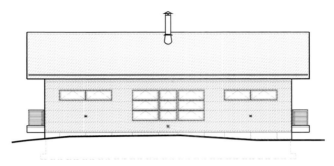

North Elevation

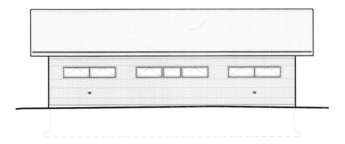

South Elevation

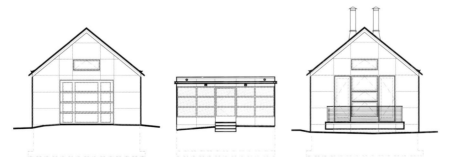

East Elevations

**Design Team of the House of Volumes**
Margaret McCurry, Stanley Tigerman, Jeremy Hinton, Megan Musgrave

**Design Team of the House of Planes**
Margaret McCurry, Stanley Tigerman, Jeremy Hinton, Rachel Oleinick

**Interior Design of the House of Volumes**
Margaret McCurry, Megan Musgrave

**Interior Design of the House of Planes**
Mary Luby, Mary Luby Interior Design, Inc.

**Lighting Design**
Darrell Hawthorne, Architecture & Light

**Landscape Design**
Hoerr Schaudt Landscape Architects

**General Contractor**
Lakeshore Enterprises

**Photographer**
Steve Hall, Hedrich Blessing Photographers

# THE HOUSE OF PLANES,
# THE HOUSE OF VOLUMES

HARBOR COUNTRY, MICHIGAN
2011

Located on a sandy bluff overlooking Lake Michigan's southeastern shore, these two 7,000-square-foot homes expand an existing historic family compound that dates to the early 20th century. The Chicago clients desired sophisticated yet sustainable designs that would incorporate the amenities associated with their urban lifestyles into these more relaxed country retreats.

Working jointly, Tigerman and McCurry chose to approach the houses as two distinct variations on a common theme, which would standardize details and allow for construction staging between the two homes. The houses were sited such that each family would inhabit its own private space while the terraced land between the homes would become a central gathering site for the extended family. Since the land slopes towards the bluff, the first floors of the houses are stepped incrementally to follow the contours. A field stone path axially bisects this terraced area and terminates in a council ring or fire pit reminiscent of a favorite feature employed by Jens Jensen, the original landscape architect for the property. The partners also worked with the Michigan Department of Environmental Quality to carefully locate the houses to prevent dune erosion. The plans incorporate wood boardwalks to traverse critical dune areas so that these slopes are preserved.

The two houses are each designed with a two-story central circulation "spline" that is flanked by living spaces. While acting as a transparent reveal between the forms, the spline contains the stairway, thereby interconnecting the levels and linking the ground floor to family rooms below ground. Entry for each home is centered on the glazed spline, which sets up axial views through the double-height spaces onto rear patios and the lake beyond while flooding the stairwells with natural light.

While each house is clad in mimetic materials, a rain screen of Port Orford cedar and white composite aluminum panels, each is also uniquely different in its material expression. For one of them, the "House of Planes," the exterior walls are articulated such that they rise above and beyond the main volume of the structure while the floor planes extend beyond the walls to create deep balconies and overhangs. The house also shifts materials at each end to emphasize the "slipped" planes. Its counterpoint is the "House of Volumes," which is just that, stacked cubistic forms that are differentiated materially between the first and second stories.

The partners designed both homes to incorporate a variety of sustainable features. The homes feature low-VOC foam insulation used in conjunction with cellulose with a high recycled content to achieve a high R-value. A geothermal heating and cooling system, which uses ground water as a heat source, is also used by the two new homes and was added to the existing family home, which had also been previously remodeled by the partners. Other features include solar panels to provide domestic hot water, radiant heat flooring on the interior and green roof plantings. These, coupled with the use of natural materials and fabrics, contribute to a healthful sustainable environment.

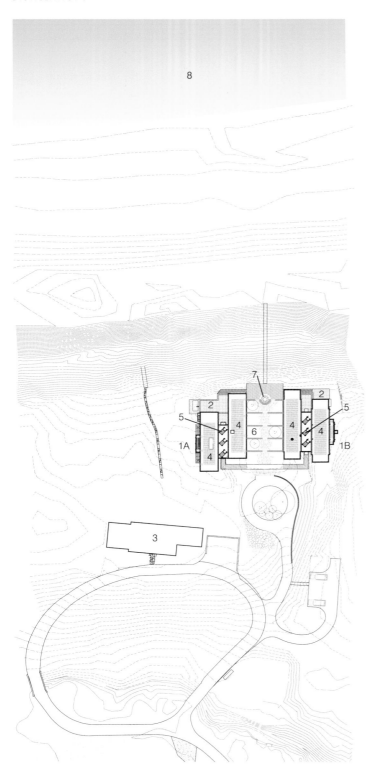

Site Plan
1a House of Volumes
1b House of PLanes
2 Terrace
3 Existing Residence
4 Green Roofs
5 Solar Panels
6 Greensward
7 Fire Pit
8 Lake Michigan

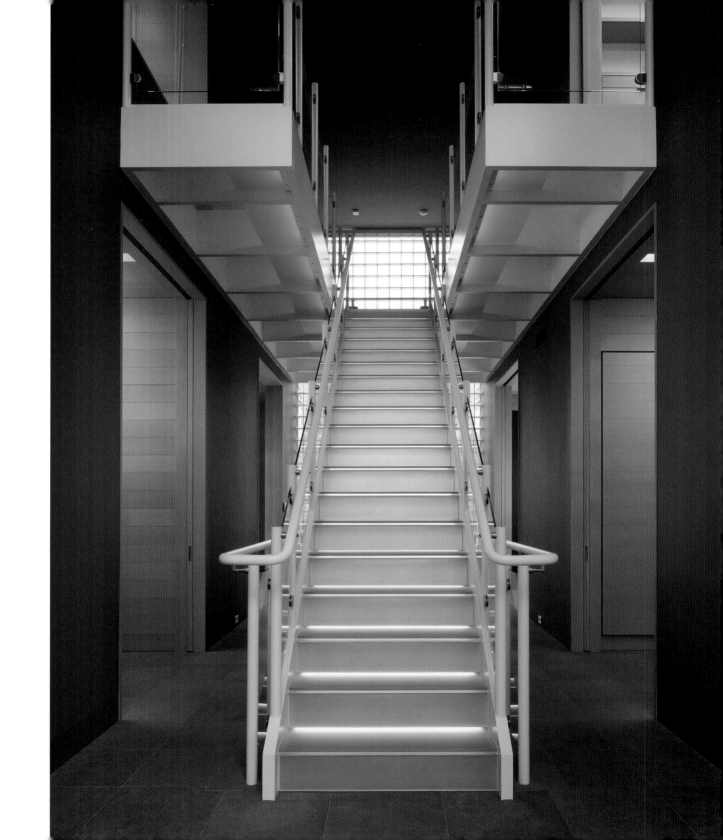

Illuminated Photograph by Ellen Galinsky

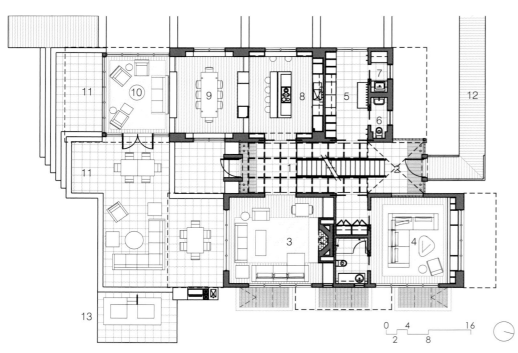

House of Volumes
First-Floor Plan
1 Stair Hall
2 Foyer
3 Living Room
4 Den
5 Mudroom
6 Powder Room
7 Utility Room
8 Kitchen
9 Dining Room
10 Sun Room
11 Terrace
12 Boardwalk

House of Volumes
Second-Floor Plan
 1  Stair Hall
 2  Master Bedroom
 3  Dressing
 4  Master Bath
 5  Study
 6  Balcony
 7  Children's Room
 8  Bunkroom
 9  Guest Room
10  Bathroom

House of Planes
First-Floor Plan
1   Stair Hall
2   Foyer
3   Den
4   Guest Bedroom and Bath
5   Mudroom
6   Kitchen
7   Living and Dining Room
8   Sunroom
9   Terrace
10  Boardwalk

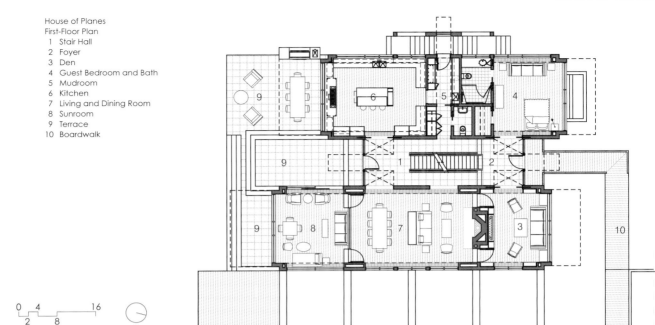

Opposite and Facing Pages: Furnishing selection by Mary Luby of Mary Luby Interior Design, Inc.

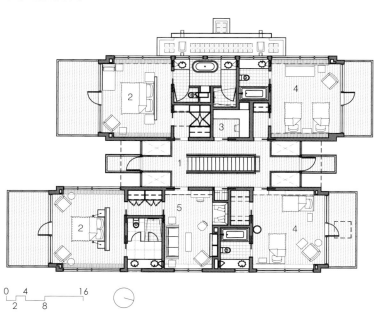

House of Planes
Second-Floor Plan
1  Stair Hall
2  Master Bedroom
3  Office
4  Guest Bedroom and Bath
5  Family Room

0  4    16
  2   8

Opposite and Facing Pages: Furnishing selection by Mary Luby of Mary Luby Interior Design, Inc.

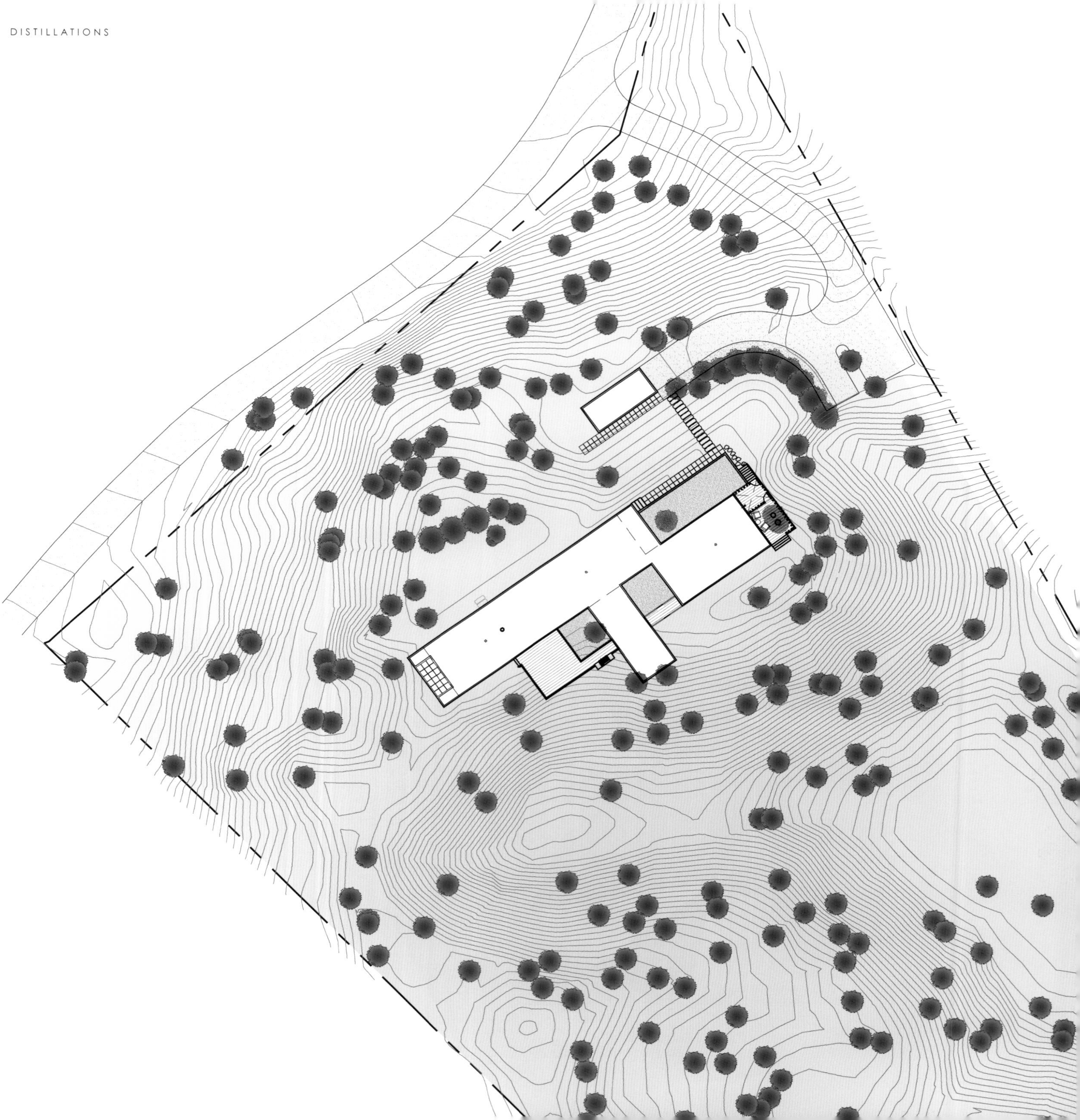

# THE HOUSE ON THE RIDGE

SOUTHWESTERN MICHIGAN
2012

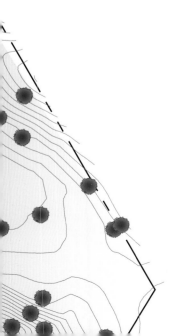

**Design Team**
Margaret McCurry, Jeremy Hinton, Erik Martin,
Harold DiVito

**Interior Design**
Margaret McCurry and Owners

**Lighting Design**
Tigerman McCurry Architects

A gravel road runs in a dale between the sandy dunes formed by the prevailing westerly winds that blow across Lake Michigan. The House of Five Gables is sited on a knoll on the lake side of this country lane. Across the road and up the opposing dune, this metal and glass house will spread out along a forested ridge that overlooks yet another series of hills and dales stretching inland towards the cultivated flat farmland to the east.

In contradistinction to the red house's distinctly vernacular design, a distillation of the essence of rural barns in the region, this white house eschews such referentiality in favor of geometric abstraction. Raised on a narrow plinth that detaches the house from the land the horizontal window mullions reinforce its linearity while establishing a regularized grid not unlike those employed by its Mid-Century Modernist antecedents. However, its differentiated column bay distinguishes it from its owners' favorite old master, the Farnsworth House by Mies van der Rohe. As a masterpiece of the modern movement , Edith Farnsworth's house has no equal and so, while the House on the Ridge was deliberately designed in the spirit of the original, "floating" its core and detailing all components minimally following Mies' purported statement that "God is in the details", it is in no way mimetic. It attempts in its own way to reestablish the tradition initially accomplished by Greek architects in their temple designs. Those paradigms sit upon a plinth detached from the land separating man and his constructs from nature and, in a way, positing mind over matter.

The owners of the House on the Ridge will enjoy unobstructed views of the landscape in all seasons. They will watch the sun rise and set over the hills in the winter and, sheltered by tall oaks in the summer, enjoy cool breezes wafting across their decks. In the evening the house will become a lantern guiding friends and neighbors along the road to a warm welcome in this modern aerie.

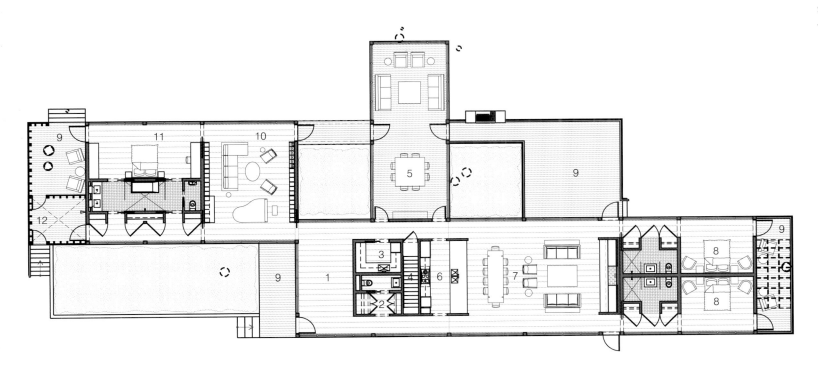

First-Floor Plan
1 Foyer
2 Powder Room and Closet
3 Pantry
4 Stair
5 Screened Porch
6 Kitchen
7 Living and Dining Room
8 Guest Bedroom and Bath
9 Deck
10 Den
11 Master Bedroom Suite
12 Outdoor Shower

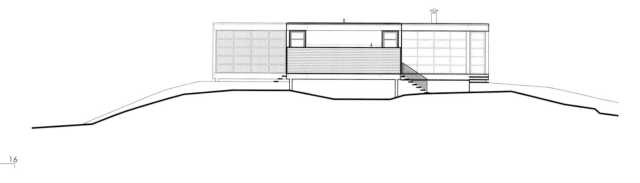

0  4      16
  2    8

East elevation

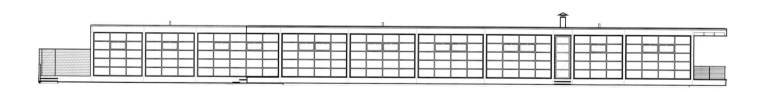

0  4      16
  2    8

North elevation

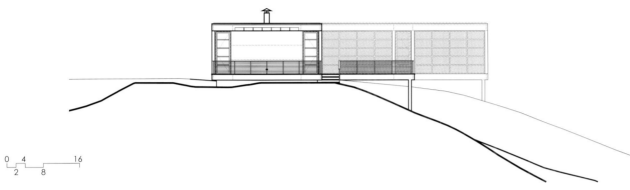

0  4      16
  2   8

West elevation

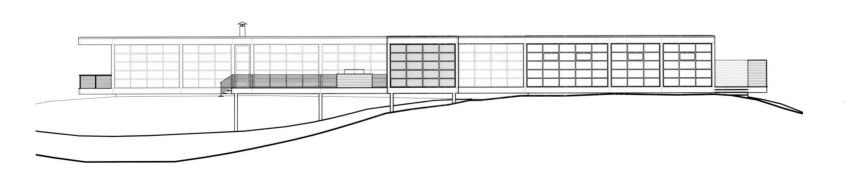

0  4      16
  2   8

South elevation

# BIOGRAPHY

MARGARET MCCURRY is president and a principal of the distinguished Chicago architecture firm, Tigerman McCurry Architects. McCurry, a native Chicagoan and Fellow of the American Institute of Architects, received her Bachelor's degree in Art History from Vassar College and her Loeb Fellowship in Advanced Environmental Studies from the Graduate School of Design at Harvard University. Well-known for synthesizing the American vernacular with Classical Modernism, her award-winning projects have been published widely in architectural and interior magazines and exhibited at museums and galleries both in the United States and abroad. McCurry has lectured at many architectural and design conferences, as well as schools of architecture and design at major universities, and has taught design studios in addition to authoring articles for architectural journals and catalogs.

# PHOTOGRAPHY CREDITS

Christopher Barrett © Hedrich Blessing: 9, 54, 57, 63, 64, 67, 68, 69, 70, 71, 72; courtesy Architectural Digest © The Condé Nast Publications; all rights reserved; used with permission: 34

Craig Dugan © Hedrich Blessing: 89, 91, 92, 93, 95

Steve Hall © Hedrich Blessing: 2, 11, 12, 13, 26, 29, 30, 32, 33, 34, 35, 36, 37, 46, 49, 50, 51, 52, 53, 58, 59, 60, 61, 62, 78, 80, 81, 82, 83, 84, 85, 86, 87, 104, 107, 108, 109, 113, 114, 115, 116, 117, 118, 123, 124, 125, 126, 132, 133, 142, 145, 146, 148, 149, 150, 151, 152, 154, 156, 157, 158, 159, 160, 163, 165, 166, 167, 168, 169, 210, 213, 215, 216, 217, 218, 219, 220, 221, 222, 223, 224, 225, 226, 227, 228, 229, 230, 231, 232, 233, 240; courtesy Architectural Digest © The Condé Nast Publications; all rights reserved; used with permission: 94, 96, 97, 110, 111, 112, 122, 127, 147, 153, 162, 164,

Timothy Hursley, courtesy Architectural Digest © The Condé Nast Publications; all rights reserved; used with permission: 74, 76,

Margaret McCurry: 119, 120, 121, 122, 125, 127

Jon Miller © Hedrich Blessing, courtesy Architectural Digest © The Condé Nast Publications; all rights reserved; used with permission: 70, 72, 73

© Erhard Pfeiffer 2010: 12, 170, 171, 173, 174, 175, 176, 177, 178, 179, 180, 181, 182, 183, 184, 185, 186, 187

© Jim Powell Photography: 98, 100, 101, 102, 103, 188, 193, 191, 192, 194, 195, 196, 197, 198, 199

© David Seide/DefinedSpace.com: 128, 131, 134, 136, 137, 138, 139, 140, 141

Renderings:
Harold DiVito and Erik Martin: 9, 11, 13, 19, 20, 51, 52, 56, 59, 63, 69, 79, 82, 85, 90, 93, 96, 106, 111, 115, 122, 133, 136, 140, 147, 152, 166, 174, 179, 186, 200, 204, 205, 206, 207, 208, 209, 214, 222, 227, 231, 232, 238, 237, 239

Erik Martin: 12, 203

ORO *editions*
Publishers of Architecture, Art, and Design
Gordon Goff – Publisher
www.oroeditions.com
info@oroeditions.com

Distillations: The Architecture of Margaret McCurry
by Margaret McCurry with the assistance of Harold DiVito, Erik Martin and Mara Wilhelm

ISBN: 978-1-935935-06-3

Writer: Margaret McCurry
Editor and Project Manager: Gordon Goff
Art Direction and Graphic Design: Pablo Mandel / CircularStudio
Production Manager: Usana Shadday
Production Assistance: Gabriel Ely
Project Coordinator: Christy LaFaver

Designed and Produced by ORO *editions*
Color Separation and Printing: ORO *group* Ltd
Text printed using offset sheetfed printing process in 4 color
on 157gsm Premium matt artpaper.
Printed in China.

*Distillations* text is set in Century Gothic, a typeface based on Monotype 20th Century, which was drawn by Sol Hess between 1936 and 1947. Century Gothic maintains the basic design of 20th Century but has an enlarged 'x' height and has been modified to ensure satisfactory output from modern digital systems. The design is influenced by the geometric style sans serif faces which were popular during the 1920s and '30s. Useful for headlines and general display work and for small quantities of text, particularly in advertising.

Library of Congress Cataloging-in-Publication Data Available.

ORO *editions* has made every effort to minimize the overall carbon footprint of this project. As part of this goal, ORO *editions*, in association with Global ReLeaf, have arranged to plant two trees for each and every tree used in the manufacturing of the paper produced for this book. Global ReLeaf is an international campaign run by American Forests, the nation's oldest nonprofit conservation organization. Global ReLeaf is American Forests' education and action program that helps individuals, organizations, agencies, and corporations improve the local and global environment by planting and caring for trees.